Contents

Contributors

Lindsey Day

is the cofounder and editor in chief of *CRWN* magazine, a premium, independent print publication about natural hair and the women who wear it. Through beautiful content, thoughtful commentary, hair inspiration, and resources, *CRWN* exists to edify and empower Black women across the globe.

Website: crwnmag.com
Social: @crwnmag, @lindseydayy

Lora DiFranco

is the founder of Free Period Press and coauthor of *Self Care Index: A Pocket Guide for Remembering the Things You Like to Do*. She lives in Cleveland, Ohio, with her wife and houseplants.

Website: freeperiodpress.com
Social: @freeperiodpress

Erin Ellis

is an award-winning letterer and illustrator who likes drawing flowers with her eyes closed. Her client list includes Facebook, Aldo, The Body Shop, NASA, Emma Roberts, and Ceres Organics. A recovering tumbleweed, Erin lives on a farm in New Jersey and treasures her creative community.

Website: erinellis.com
Social: @leavesandletterforms

Nora Gomez-Strauss

is an arts administrator currently serving as the Public Art Fund's director of digital strategies. She lives in her native borough of Queens, New York, with her husband and two children, where they can be found going for long walks and listening to records.

Website: nogophoto.com
Social: @nogophoto

Ebony Haight

is an artist, writer, and clothing maker who lives and works in San Francisco. She's passionate about good stories well told, and beautiful things well made.

Website: heira.studio
Social: @ebonyh

Deun Ivory

is a creative visionary, brilliant photographer, multidisciplinary artist, engaging speaker, and the art director for the culture-shifting wellness brand—Black Girl In Om. Her signature aesthetic and thought-leadership has led to content creation for Nike and brand partnerships with VSCO, HBO, Netflix, and Make Up For Ever.

Website: deunivory.me
Social: @deunivory

Dream Big!

Editor's Letter

Too often we see the stories of creative people and their careers boiled down to a highlight reel. We are shown their greatest achievements, but we aren't reminded of all the moments they stumbled (and continue to)—or how they got back up again. No matter what stage of life and work you're in, *fear and failure are part of everyone's journey*. And sometimes we actually learn more from what hasn't worked out rather than what has.

So for our second issue, I wanted to jump headfirst into these topics that can make us feel uncomfortable and vulnerable. Because as intimidating as fear and failure can be, they are the issues we *need* to be discussing more openly and with more compassion—both for ourselves and for our communities as a whole.

In our last issue, we explored all the different facets and parts of our creative communities and learned an important lesson: We are stronger together.

So with this issue, let's work hand in hand to talk openly about the things that scare us. Let's form new bonds and connections as we help our communities air out the issues we're most afraid of and find the most intimidating. Because when we work together, solutions and support systems become clearer and problems become less overwhelming. There is always someone in our community who understands our experience, knows how we feel, and has an idea that can help us push through to the other side.

This issue is filled with stories of creatives who have faced challenges, asked for help, and learned new ways of looking at fear and failure that take the sting out of life's most challenging moments. I hope you'll find their stories, experiences, and advice as uplifting and reaffirming as I did. After finishing this issue, I felt a little less alone, a lot more connected, and infinitely more inspired to try harder and dream bigger. I hope you'll feel the same.

xo,

Activist and founder of Equality for HER, Blair Imani talks about facing her fears head-on and finding a balance between life online and off.

Story on p. 93

Photo by Myles Loftin

Special thanks to: Lia Ronnen, Aliena Cameron, Kelli Kehler, Caitlin Kelch, Julia Turshen, Rochelle Udell, and Doug Turshen for their support on this issue.

Kelli Hart Kehler

is the managing editor for Design*Sponge, a writer, and a journalist by trade. She managed production of Grace Bonney's book *In the Company of Women*, and also production for this second issue of *Good Company*. She lives in California with her husband and two daughters.

Social: @kellikehler

Alicia Kennedy

is a Long Island–born, Brooklyn-based food and drink writer. She is a *Village Voice* contributor and has written for the *New York Times*, the *Guardian*, *Taste*, *GQ*, and more.

Website: alicia-kennedy.com

(photo by Thosh Collins)

Chelsey Luger

is a freelance journalist and indigenous wellness advocate based in Phoenix, Arizona, originally from the Turtle Mountain Band of Chippewa and Standing Rock Sioux Tribe in North Dakota. She is a trainer for the Native Wellness Institute and the cofounder of Well For Culture, an indigenous wellness initiative.

Website: chelseyluger.com
Social: @chelsey.luger

Amanda Machado

is a writer and educator who has lived and worked around the world. Her writing about travel and identity has been published in *The Atlantic*, the *Washington Post*, *Harper's Bazaar*, Vox, the REI *Co-op Journal*, and elsewhere.

Website: amandaemachado.com
Social: @amandaemachado0

Meg José Mateo

is a writer and designer in the San Francisco Bay Area. She likes to pursue creative work that encourages innovative storytelling, shares diverse and authentic stories, and connects to multicultural and marginalized audiences.

Website: mateoilasco.com
Social: @mateoilasco

George McCalman

is an artist and creative director, born in the Caribbean, raised in New York, and currently based in San Francisco. A former art director of fourteen years, he left the editorial world to open his own creative studio. He has a monthly illustrated column, Observed, featured in the *San Francisco Chronicle*.

Website: mccalman.co
Social: @mccalmanco

Contributors

Debbie Millman

is host of Design Matters, one of the world's first and longest-running podcasts; chair of the first-ever master's in branding program at the School of Visual Arts; and the author of six books on design and branding.

Website: debbiemillman.com
Social: @debbiemillman

Kari Mugo

is an activist and writer born and raised in Nairobi, Kenya, who spent her formative years in Minnesota. She is an avid traveler, perpetual list-maker, and sometime performer. Her words have appeared on the internet, radio, and stage.

Website: thewarmfruit.squarespace.com
Twitter: @the_warm_fruit
Instagram: @thewarmfruit

Sarah Neuburger

is the fiercely optimistic freelance illustrator and owner of The Small Object, based in Atlanta, Georgia, who can fall in love with the beauty of a drawn line over and over again.

Website: sarahneuburger.com
Social: @thesmallobject

Sally Nixon

is an illustrator based in Little Rock, Arkansas. Her first book, *Houseplants and Hot Sauce: A Seek-and-Find Book for Grown-Ups*, is out now.

Website: sallynixon.com
Social: @sallustration

(photo by Clémence Polès)

Fariha Roísín

is a writer living on Earth.

Website: fariharoisin.com
Twitter: @fariharoisin
Instagram: @fariha_roisin

Elazar Sontag

loves to write about home cooking and the intersections of food, social justice, and sexuality. He is the author of *Flavors of Oakland*, and his stories appear in the *Washington Post*, Vice, and Serious Eats, among other publications.

Website: elazarsontag.com
Twitter: @elazarsontag
Instagram: @e_zar

Lauren Tamaki

is a Canadian living in Brooklyn. She worked as a designer/art director at Bumble and bumble and Kate Spade Saturday before focusing on illustration full-time. Her clients include the *New York Times, New York* magazine, Pentagram, and Penguin.

Website: laurentamaki.com
Social: @laurentamaki

TANAÏS

is the author of *Bright Lines*, a finalist for the Center for Fiction First Novel Prize, the Edmund White Award for Debut Fiction, and the Brooklyn Eagles Literary Prize. She's the founder of the independent beauty and fragrance house Hi Wildflower and host of the *Mala* podcast and perfume anthology.

Website: hiwildflower.com
Social: @hiwildflower

Jacob Tobia

is a writer, producer, and author of the forthcoming memoir *Sissy: A Coming-of-Gender Story* (Penguin Random House). A member of both the Forbes 30 Under 30 and the OUT 100, Jacob has been featured in the *New York Times, Time, New York* magazine, *Teen Vogue*, and the *Guardian*.

Website: jacobtobia.com
Social: @JacobTobia

Kayla Whaley

is a writer living outside Atlanta. Her work has appeared in Catapult and the *Michigan Quarterly Review* and on The Toast, among other venues. She'll receive her MFA from the University of Tampa in January 2019.

Website: kaylawhaley.com
Social: @PunkinOnWheels

Jenna Wortham

is a staff writer for the *New York Times Magazine* and cohost of the podcast *Still Processing*. She is the coauthor of the forthcoming visual anthology *Black Futures* with Kimberly Drew and OneWord.

Website: jennydeluxe.com
Social: @jennydeluxe

Angelica Yarde

is a graphic designer, web developer, speaker, owner of Studio 404 paper shop, and cohost of the *Heart + Hustle Podcast*. She co-owns Sevenality, a branding strategy firm, with her husband in Celebration, Florida.

Website: sevenality.com
Social: @studio404design

What is your Biggest Fear?

Group Q & A with Melissa Alam, Danielle Evans,
Marie Denee & Melissa Kimble

By Angelica Yarde
Illustrations by Lauren Tamaki

Fear is defined as an unpleasant emotion caused by the belief that someone or something is dangerous. Even in its most unpleasant form, fear allows us to make room for growth, nurturing, and preservation through the things we tend to avoid.

I asked four amazing women—freelance digital marketing strategist and photographer Melissa Alam, designer and lettering artist Danielle Evans, plus-size fashion and style expert Marie Denee, and digital and social media strategist Melissa Kimble—

about how they've dealt with fear and what it means to create without fear.

How do you define fear?

Melissa Alam: Fear is the fuel I use to test my abilities and strengths as a woman. I see fear as an obstacle that forces me to use my creativity and resources to find a solution. I definitely feel fear every day in both life and in business situations, but I don't use it to impede or slow me down. I sit myself down, think about what I'm actually afraid

of (or the worst-case scenario), and I work backward to create a plan for overcoming that gut feeling of anxiety. I've realized that in 99 percent of situations, other people have already gone through the same fears or obstacles, so there's always a way to turn that fear into a win!

Danielle Evans: I'd define fear as the squirming between the unknown, looming future and the predictable failures of the past. I've noticed a strange paradox: Our fears often hinge on positive expansion, the opportunities we encounter to better ourselves. Rather than seeing new challenges as a means to gain, we tend to focus on the worst-case scenario, losing and experiencing a negative shift in the status quo. This is strange, considering people with gambling addictions approach card tables with the belief that they have everything to gain even when the odds are stacked against them to lose. If only we had an ounce of their confidence! I tend to recollect times I attempted to expand and circumstances forced me to shrink. This tension is normal. Nobody has hard-and-fast shortcuts around this discomfort, but everyone can opt to engage their insecurities in a productive way.

Marie Denee: False Evidence Appearing Real. LOL. Also, I use fear as fuel to drive me to chase my goals. I always have fear, and it is not always a bad thing. It can go one way or the other . . .

Fear can inspire or immobilize you, and I try to use my fear to drive me to my next level—whatever it is.

Melissa Kimble: Fear is being afraid of something that may or may not be tangible. It's the direct opposite of love.

What was one time you were able to turn fear into opportunity?

Melissa Alam: I was recently at SXSW in Austin and attended an amazing event held by Bumble. They had a pitch competition, and of course, the typical good angel/bad angel routine went through my head. "Your idea isn't even fully developed." "There's no chance you'll win." "You've never pitched anything before!"

But I also told myself, "What's the worst that can happen?" I practiced my pitch in my head for a business idea I've had for over five years now and just went for it. I ended up winning, which validated the concept that you miss all the shots you don't take. I'm never missing another opportunity, moving forward, because of exactly this experience!

Danielle Evans: When my work first began gaining traction back in 2014, my "studio" was a wooden board atop a trash can next to my desk. I could only work during favorable daylight conditions because I only shot in natural light. I realized moving was the only option if I wanted to grow, but I had conditions: Since most of my lettering is assembled and shot top-down, I needed enough space for three simultaneous projects, ample windows, high white ceilings to reflect light, and storage space, since I also planned to invest in more equipment. When I'd found the right place, I was scared and a little sticker shocked; I'd doubled my living space as well as my rent.

However, within a week I had a handful of projects that satisfied the financial risk and assured me I'd made the right decision.

A graver example: My marriage dissolved back in late 2016. I sensed that the end of my decade-long relationship was looming and worried about the ramifications of heartache on my career. I'd worked so hard to stabilize my art and establish myself. If the depression and subsequent stress on my finances, relationships, and spirit battered me to hell, could I sustain myself long enough to recover? After thinking long and hard, I knew I could survive this tumultuous shift, but I'd have to prioritize my health, and acknowledge any fears and pain while continuing to press forward.

Sometimes I'd take weeks off at a time, travel, hit up my therapist. Other weeks I was maniacally working, channeling my emotions into art. The turning point that ultimately tipped my decision to move on was this: I'd been sloughing through status quo for a while, and it was debilitating, already painful. What if better times rather than worse were on the other side? I made lists of dreams, life decisions I'd make. I took responsibility for my poor decision-making that had led me here and empowered myself to advocate, educate, and strengthen myself for every possible outcome. A year later, I wrote about these lessons to help empower others in a similar place of grief. Not only did I receive many messages of solidarity and encouragement from others in similar spaces, but I also received client thanks for pushing through my grief to make our collaborations the best I could. The validation was immense! Happy to report I'm in a much better space, both personally and professionally.

Marie Denee: My TCFStyle Expo! I had been afraid of taking this idea and making it into a reality. Four years later, here we are with a two-day plus-size shopping and social event, catering to both the plus-size woman and the Big & Tall man! For me, it has allowed me the chance to take my vision and turn it into a reality, to scale the business on a different level and to engage our readers with a completely immersive plus-size fashion experience!

Melissa Kimble: When I was unexpectedly laid off from my job at a national publication in Chicago, it created an opportunity for me to take a new direction in my career. I was super scared to leave the comfort of my hometown, but it allowed me to create a new professional vision for myself in New York City.

What could you create in your life if fear weren't an issue?

Melissa Alam: If fear weren't an issue, anything could be possible! I would go all in to grow my businesses and bring on a full team to scale and go national. I'd take more risks when it comes to investing in people, my time, and equipment, and I wouldn't look back. The sky's the limit when it comes to achieving your goals and creating your best life.

Danielle Evans: I'd create more space to exercise my opinion through my work. Growing up I was unfiltered, and that hurt people. Now when I communicate, I deliver my thoughts assertively and use confident, direct language; my vocal tone considerably softens my take, but when disembodied through writing, I can sound harsh. In recent years I've corrected myself, and in some cases overcorrected, to be more accessible. However, that accessibility comes with a price. I'm always reminding myself that communicating directly is the best way to attract the right people into my life. The one certainty is in not pleasing everybody and trusting this is okay.

Marie Denee: If fear were not an issue? Ohhhhh . . . Girl, I would aim for becoming an Oprah-level media brand. I would grow out my video, make this office/headquarters dream a reality, and take more

risks! I am slowly working on these things, but at times I think my fear of success slows me down, right? I am on this curious journey where I am learning more and more about myself as a woman, business owner, and OG in the plus-size blogging space . . . Right now, I am learning who I am and learning how to *stand* in that.

Melissa Kimble: If fear weren't an issue, I'd create more opportunities for others to do what they love, especially those who are in positions where they can't "afford" to do what they love.

Pursuing your purpose and your passion is also a privilege and I'd love for more people from low-income and underserved communities to get the opportunity to do that as well.

What is one suggestion you have for facing fears?

Melissa Alam: Find a supportive group of friends or colleagues who you trust who can help you figure out solutions to your fear or just talk them out with you. I've always had this *lone wolf* mentality when it comes to making decisions (#TypeA PersonalityProblems), but I've realized that most of my anxiety and fear can be faced if I just ask for help or open up to those around me.

Also, I would suggest everyone attend my yearly conference, FearlessCon (FearlessCon.com)! It's held every fall in Philadelphia and is a space for ambitious, diverse women and non-binary people to feel empowered, have their voices be heard, and leave inspired to kick ass when it comes to life and business. This year it'll be September 29th and 30th, and I can't wait

to inspire a fearless attitude and mind-set in everyone who attends!

Danielle Evans: Fears can be combated by education and acknowledgment. I've worried about upgrading camera equipment, a necessity every couple of years. I don't love the photographic aspect of my job anyway, so responsibly sinking money into a new body or light feels heavier than other tasks. However, I read online reviews and ask a thousand questions at the camera store. I test models and compare lenses, consider used refurbishments, crunch numbers to determine if I should buy vs. rent when needed. Ultimately I know nicer equipment will pay for itself, but I'm lessening all the variables and locking down the constants until I reach a decision.

Am I freaked out by so many dollar signs? Definitely, but I won't allow myself to be hindered. There's too much to be done.

Marie Denee: Have an amazing support system or network of like-minded folks who help push you beyond and through your fears. To have that accountability will give you no choice but to face and power through those fears. And as a woman of faith, prayer. Prayer and faith help me actualize my goals, dreams, and purpose to attack those fears!

Melissa Kimble: Get used to feeling afraid—it never goes away. If you're constantly pushing the envelope, you'll always come face-to-face with your fears. Once you accept it as part of the journey, it's easy to see it as a reaction to you taking a step forward instead of something that should hold you back. **gc**

IDENTIFYING AS ME

Activist and writer Jacob Tobia talks to comic, actor, and producer Rhea Butcher about how gender and gender identity connect to life on and off stage.

Photography by Oriana Koren
Lettering by Samantha Hahn

When famed lesbian comic Rhea Butcher decided it was time to publicly disclose their non-binary identity, they did so the way any self-respecting comedian would: via a chain of tweets. It started in January—"I'm non-binary but I identify WITH women"—revved up in February—"If you think it's like all chill to be non-binary/lesbian these days, watch me walk past a high school alone"—and continued through March— "FYI I use they/them/their pronouns now."

From the get-go, Butcher's non-binary coming out didn't play by the rules of a typical celebrity "coming-out moment." There were a few headlines and blog items covering the news, but there certainly wasn't a press release or publicity tour. In Butcher's own (tweeted) words, "I held off having some 'press release' style thing because

A. I didn't want to because I want the attention to be on comedy, my work, etc. and B. People can be needlessly cruel."

Emblazoned with the disclaimer "No publicists were involved in the making of this gender," their coming-out moment was less of *a moment* and more of an incremental unfurling. What their public disclosure lacked in drama and noise, it made up for in grace. Too gradual about the whole thing to really make a splash, a splash wasn't what they were going for in the first place. Instead, Butcher opted for a series of gradual ripples, a stone skittering across the surface of the water before gently gliding in.

And isn't this what coming out *should be*, anyway? Isn't this what non-binary people deserve? The opportunity to simply glide into our gender, to effortlessly own it, to arrive at a place of happiness and self-actualization, fanfare optional?

Six months into their unfurling, Rhea Butcher sat down with me, resident non-binary trans-femme cutie, to discuss the state of comedy, Ford F-150s, weird midwestern roots, and, of course, all things genderfabulous.

I'm so excited to have the chance to chat, because when I was living in New York there were visible non-binary people *everywhere*. And I feel like now that I'm in Los Angeles, there are still non-binary people everywhere, but I don't find them as easily.

They're hiding in their houses, because *everybody's* hiding in their houses in Los Angeles.

We're just in our cars and we're passing each other on the freeway and we don't see each other.

Yeah, exactly. Can I also just point out that "non-binary" sounds like, you know, "I don't work in the bookbinding factory anymore"?

Like, "I don't have *any* binding."

"I'm not binding *anything* anymore." I'm binding *myself*, but not material things.

Publicly using the language of "non-binary" is kind of new for you, right?

Kind of, yeah.

But is it privately new for you?

Like, new-*ish*. I mean, I always related to genderqueer, gender-nonconforming, and stuff like that. And butch. It's all within the same family of terminology, right? It's all contextual, and whatever you want it to mean is kinda what it means. So it *is* new for me in that—despite the amount of theory that I've gone through in my own life and taking women's studies back when it was still *called* "women's studies"—oh god, now I'm just aging myself. I'm saying "women's studies" because I am three hundred years old.

You're a dinosaur. You're Ben Franklin.

Yeah, exactly. I took women's studies and I also took queer theory classes, but that was in 2003 in Akron, Ohio. And the language

even then was very different from what it is now. It's all an evolution, and I *sort of* feel like it's new to me but only because I just didn't know the word *non-binary* back then.

For me, it isn't "coming out of the closet," necessarily; it's just finding a new aspect of myself. There are many people who feel that they came out of the closet about being a non-binary person. But I feel like I came out of the closet as a lesbian, as a gay person, as a homosexual when I did. And that was the moment that I "came out of the closet" and I smashed it and got rid of it after that, you know?

Whereas now I feel like it's just a new level or plateau or something. You're on a path and you get to a high point and you look out and you go, "Oh, *non-binary*. That makes a lot of sense for me now." That's how I relate to my experience. It's less of "I've thought this for a long time and now I'm telling all of you." You know what I mean?

Yeah, I like to talk about my non-binary journey as an open archaeological dig where a bunch of tourists were walking by the whole time, looking in. And I'm not a very good archaeologist. I've broken a lot of things and fucked up a lot of priceless artifacts in the process.

Yes. Some teeth got pitched into the trash.

When you were doing the disclosure process, talking about yourself as non-binary for the first time—

You mean my ingrate tweet storm?

Makeup by Rachael Vang

Yes, your ingrate tweet storm, the veritable hurricane. You said you were apprehensive about what your comedy pal colleagues would say about it. What was behind that anxiety?

It's mostly just the people that think pronouns are a joke. As a person who was following in the footsteps of other queer comedians—even specifically my wife, Cameron Esposito—just talking about "being gay" onstage, people would roll their eyes, like, "Oh, look at this *social justice warrior* . . ."

The reason I talk about this stuff is because that's what my life is. I want to tell other comedians, "*You're* talking about stuff that you think everybody relates to. It's become neutral *for you*, so it's totally fine. You don't even see it as *of your own experience* anymore."

I think that was my anxiety. I don't necessarily want my comedy career to be like, "Oh, you've become *the* non-binary spokesperson!" I guess I'm fine with being *the* non-binary comic for now, but I don't want that to be the only thing that people think of when they think of me. I *also* want them to think that I'm, I don't know, smart and funny.

There's no need for either of us to "speak for" the non-binary community.

Sure, yeah. When I'm speaking in a mainstream space, I'm happy to speak *to* it—but I don't want it to be like, I'm the authority on this. I'm happy to be *an* authority when there is no one else non-binary in the room.

There's this perception right now, and I don't know exactly where it came

from or how we got it, but there's this perception out there that the moment you name yourself as non-binary, you're all of a sudden *fragile*.

Yeah. That's probably it, too. I'm just a snowflake now.

Like a delicate porcelain fucking vase.

Like, "Oh, I'm so sensitive 'cause I spent *so much* time like looking inward on these things . . ." You know what I mean?

Right. Right.

It's like, "No, man, I fucking worked at the back of an oven, screen printing in Akron, Ohio, and I was thinking about these things." You know?

Right. There's this idea that non-binary people only exist on fucking Fifth Avenue and in Upper East Side apartments.

Just because a lot of queer people move to the coast looking for, I don't want to say a *better* life, but maybe a *slightly more accessible* life, that's not to say that you can't have a good life, that you can't survive and thrive, in other places. You can. I've been to those places in this country.

The thing is, we exist everywhere, it's just that there's a higher concentration of us in [cities like Los Angeles and New York] because there's a higher concentration of people in these places. And then the attention goes to those places because they're media centers. It's like, "Where's the megaphone?" Of course *that's* where will get the

most attention. But I lived in Akron, Ohio, much longer than I lived in Los Angeles.

So I think, also, there's this weird perception that if you have the time to consider your gender identity or look into it at all, then you *must* be rich. You *must* have the time to do it. And it's like, "No." I know plenty of people who are non-binary and are not rich. Also, I am not rich. I don't live in some high-rise. I drive the same car I left Ohio in.

Your "indulgent" gender identity makes people think that you must also have an indulgent lifestyle.

Of course. It's *so* indulgent *[insert eyeroll]*.

No, it's actually just awareness. There are [non-binary] people that you're running into every day that you don't know are non-binary, 'cause they're not walking around yelling it and you're not paying that much attention. Which leads me to believe that it's not that big of a deal. I mean, it *is* a big deal, but it's also not that big of a deal. All you have to do is go, "Oh, that's who you are? You're non-binary? Great. Cool. Awesome, I'm into it." That's it. That's all I'm asking for: that we interact with each other with the minimal amount of dignity where everybody can just go along with their day.

I find that when people are stressed about *my* gender identity, it's because it's affecting their perception of *their own* gender identity. If you fit into a binary, if you fit into the system that already exists and that works for you, great. I'm happy about it because you feel good. But me saying "This is who I am" shouldn't affect you if you feel good where you're at, you know?

"I FIND THAT WHEN PEOPLE ARE STRESSED ABOUT MY GENDER IDENTITY, IT'S BECAUSE IT'S AFFECTING THEIR PERCEPTION OF THEIR OWN GENDER IDENTITY."

"I AM FIGHTING FOR THIS GROUP AND THEY ARE FIGHTING FOR ME. SO YOU HAVE TO TAKE ALL OF US. YOU CAN'T JUST TAKE ONE."

—Rhea Butcher

Right. We get each other.

We do.

And us uniting under the flag of non-binary doesn't mean that we're saying, "Oh, we are synonymous." It's us saying, "We are both invested in the same type of gender liberation."

Absolutely. Yes.

And our needs are different. But that's okay.

It *is* okay. Because I appreciate the needs that you have, and you appreciate the needs that I have. And so when someone is saying, "You know, I don't care about *Jacob's* needs, I only care about *your* needs," I will say, "I don't wanna work with you."

That's how that works. You just go like, "My needs are intertwined with my colleagues' needs and my community's needs. So if your concern is only about this one group, then we're gonna need to have a longer conversation. Because I am fighting for this group and they are fighting for me. So you have to take all of us. You can't just take one." I'm a big fan of kicking the door open and holding it open for other people to come in as opposed to being like, "Okay, I'll get in first and then, in a couple of years, y'all will follow me in." That's just not how it works.

Do you have any fond reminiscences of your butch Akron days?

Sure, I mean all my Akron days were butch, that's for sure. People called me a tomboy growing up and stuff like that. My grandfather was a teamster. My dad worked with sheet metal, so I was riding in hand-me-down Ford F-150s. I was shut out of most of the other [masculine] stuff. I got a little bit, like when I would drive the riding lawn mower around for fun. They would just start the thing up and put me on it. That was what I had as a toy to play with. It was the lawn mower.

And then my mom worked at *JOANN Fabric.*

Oh. My. God.

Like, my whole childhood was the most binary possible thing you can imagine. And my grandmother was super into quilting and stuff. At the time, I didn't want to be part of the quilting/seamstress thing, and now I think, *Man, I wish I would have learned that.* It was internalized misogyny and, you know, disdain for femininity that made me say, "I don't wanna quilt. No thanks." And now I'm like, "Oh man, quilting is a *skill.*" Just a skill.

I think some of my anxiety [about coming out as non-binary] was that I felt like I was giving up my womanness, something I had spent many years coming to terms with. The fact that I was and am understood as a woman in this world. But coming out as non-binary doesn't erase that from my life. It actually just makes me a fuller person: I'm identifying as the person I've always wanted to be. It helped me see that the fight for women's rights can actually be benefited a lot by speaking in gender-neutral terms.

My vision is for you to one day take up quilting and make some really good Ford F-150–themed quilts.

Yeah, dude. Absolutely. That's my dream. We can make this happen. **gc**

The Resistance

Meet the women turning fear into joy through the power of song.

By Nora Gomez-Strauss
Photography by Erin Patrice O'Brien

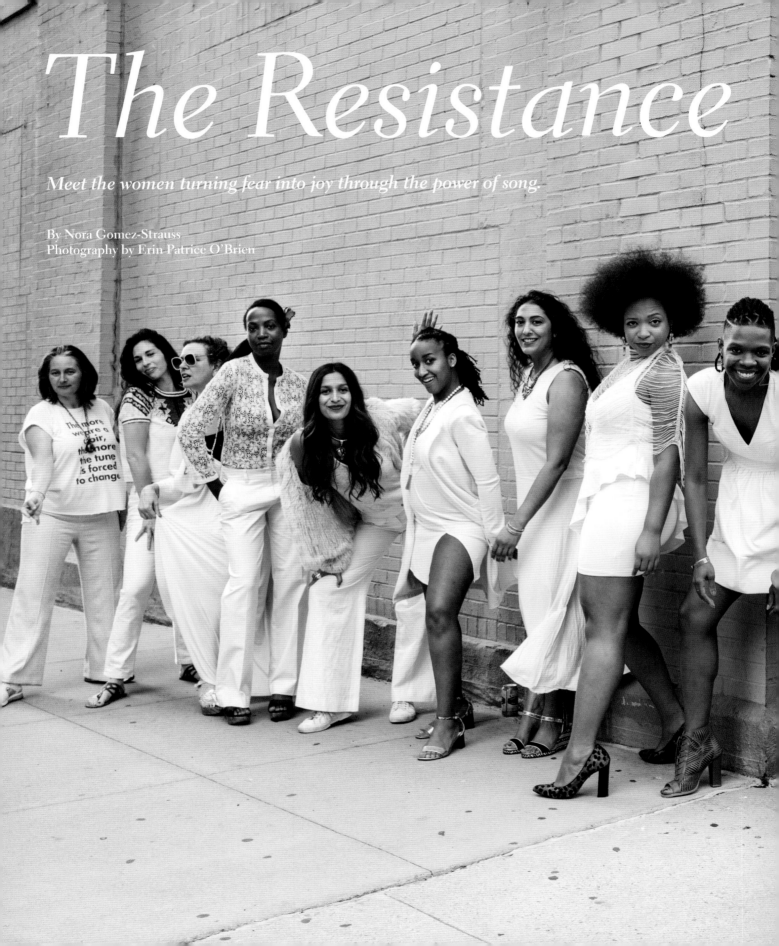

Revival Chorus

We knew that bringing women together in song is an act of resistance. We refuse to live in fear or silence.

Imagine joy. What is "joy" to you? Feeling the warmth of the sun. Eating something delicious. Hearing your child laugh. Singing along to a song you love. An emotion so exuberant that in times of upheaval or despair, experiencing and sharing joy is an act of defiance. Once a month, a collective of sixty women come together to sing as an act of resistance, spreading joy to all those who see and hear them while echoing music of protest movements that long preceded them.

This is the Resistance Revival Chorus.

The chorus was founded in the summer of 2017, emerging both directly and indirectly from the Women's March, by Sarah Sophie Flicker, Shruti Ganguly, Alyssa Klein, Jenna Lauter, Paola Mendoza, Nelini Stamp, and Ginny Suss. Their first performance took place in July 2017 at the crossroads of the world, Times Square. The flash mob sang Anne Feeney's protest song "The Rich Man's House," amending the final verse to directly address President Donald Trump. Since then, their performances have become more regular, including monthly Resistance Revival Nights, held in different spaces throughout New York City, where musical guests are invited to sing resistance songs with the group. Each night starts with a video tracing the history of resistance music from songs of the enslaved to the women's liberation movement to hip-hop, reminding us how long the tradition has existed. "The idea of protest music isn't dead—it never has been," says founding member Ginny Suss. Hosts read off recent cultural and political victories throughout the night to

cheers from the audience, and each evening is dedicated to supporting a different cause. The exuberance from the women in white on the stage radiates through and permeates the crowd, and it is difficult to find a face without a smile on it.

For so many who attend, these gatherings are not just a break from everyday life, but an about-face from a world of seemingly never-ending devastating news. It is soothing to gather and organize for change, turning anger and frustration into action—it's also cathartic to gather and lift one another's voices, to feel pure joy. Through their song and action, the chorus is always reinforcing its adage that art and culture change hearts and minds, and that joy in itself is an act of resistance.

What is the Resistance Revival Chorus? How did it come to be? What is its aim?

Sarah Sophie Flicker, Founding Member: Many of our founders have been organizing for years. The election through last summer was a particularly hectic and tiring time. Nelini Stamp and I were marching for "A Day Without a Woman." Nelini has a beautiful singing voice and was leading the crowd in song. She and I talked a few days later and recognized that we needed more music in the movement. So much of the work of repressive regimes and authoritarianism revolves around fear and silencing. We knew that bringing women together in song is an act of resistance. We refuse to live in fear or silence.

Paola Mendoza, Founding Member: We started the chorus in the summer 2017 in

response to the Trump presidency. The Resistance Revival Chorus is a collective of more than fifty women who join together to breathe joy and song into the resistance, and to uplift and center women's voices. The great artist and activist Harry Belafonte once said, "when the movement is strong, the music is strong." In that spirit we gather in community to rejuvenate our spirits and honor the protest songs that have historically been central to civil rights movements. We believe that art and culture are essential to changing hearts, minds, and history, and we commit to the principle that joy is in itself an act of resistance.

What brought you to Resistance Revival Chorus?

Shruti Ganguly, Founding Member: I'm a filmmaker, and a few years ago I had the opportunity to be on a committee of entertainment creatives and execs for the Obama administration. We were reminded of the power of media and the potential for the work we were doing, and I felt really empowered by what such stories could do to push the conversation forward. But the results of the 2016 election absolutely stunned me, along with everyone else. We had failed. Months later, I had a project premiering at Sundance; however, I decided to delay my trip to go to the Women's March in DC. There, my feeling of *Now what?* became . . . *Now this!* I then connected with Paola Mendoza and Sarah Sophie Flicker, who had been involved with the march, and met up with them for a coffee and essentially asked what I could do to help and what we could do together. And they mentioned the idea of a movement around music, and next thing I knew, we were in Sarah Sophie's kitchen, with Nelini, Ginny, Alyssa, and Jenna, having the first conversation about what would become the Resistance Revival Chorus.

Jenna Lauter, Founding Member: I work in government and politics, but grew up training to be a classical ballet dancer. I have always appreciated the unique power of art to move the soul and tap into our shared humanity in a more profound way than logic and facts can. After working on the Hillary for America campaign, I became one of the national organizers of the Women's March, where I met Ginny, Paola, and Alyssa. The Women's March put art front and center and reminded me what a force artists and the feelings they elicit can be for social change. The Resistance Revival Chorus not only strives to build awareness about pressing social issues, but also to break through the anxiety and isolation that sometimes characterize today's culture. I believe the joy, community, and hope we offer to our audiences are the antidote many of us need in this environment to keep going and working toward the world we want to create.

Nelini Stamp, Founding Member: I'm a political organizer for the Working Families Party and have been a part of many recent movements, including Occupy Wall Street. I also grew up tap dancing and singing. Since Occupy, I have been writing movement songs and learning new movement songs like "Mr. Auctioneer" that

we used at Organizing for Occupation and other movements to actively stop foreclosures. To me, music is both needed for resistance and a tool and tactic to be used in direct action. After "A Day Without a Woman," Sarah Sophie and I got together to talk about building cabaret-style nights into the resistance. Sarah Sophie pulled together a meeting around her kitchen table with Shruti, Alyssa, Ginny, Paola, and Jenna, and the Resistance Revival Chorus was born.

Ginny Suss, Founding Member: I've been a producer in the creative space for years. Music has always driven me. I've been a DJ, a tour manager, a show producer, an artist manager, a curator—all of this has led me to want to bring my eclectic set of skills to the chorus. The intersection of music/ the arts and social justice is a space where I think real change happens. I think music opens up the possibility for what could be; it offers a creative space to imagine a possible future. More than anything, to me, the chorus is about a strong sense of sisterhood and collaboration with brilliant women. It's a real life embodiment of living, breathing, intersectional feminism. We represent so many different kinds of women—different races, ethnicities, religions, socioeconomic backgrounds, people from different countries, different language speakers, LGBTQIA+ members. I believe this chorus is a wonderful opportunity to center voices of women of color, queer women, and other historically marginalized voices.

Arin Maya Lawrence, Chorus Member: I think it was a need to connect with

like-minded people at a time when so many things that were divisive in nature had been happening in the world. I remember feeling like I didn't know who my allies were or who my enemies were. When the opportunity came to join a group of women—specifically women who were boldly speaking out about several important issues and gathering in solidarity, in song!—I leapt at the chance.

Sally Rumble, Chorus Member: The chorus is a combination of my two favorite things: activism and singing. I live to do both.

What was your first experience with the group?

Sally Rumble: My very first experience was showing up at Megha's house a few hours before the Times Square flash mob action that launched us. I was delighted to see faces I already knew but had no idea were connected to the chorus (that's the tiny world of activism). I missed the earlier rehearsals so I learned the songs in my living room and while commuting beforehand. Luckily, many of the spirituals and civil rights songs aren't new to me, because I used to sing with a gospel choir at Middle Church, a church rooted in arts and activism.

Shaina Taub: I saw the first concert as an audience member before I joined the chorus. I just remember the stunning group of women entering dressed all in white and launching into "*We who believe in freedom cannot rest,*" and I felt my soul light up.

Shruti Ganguly: *Alive.* It's how we feel when we sing, it reminds us to breathe through the words that come from a deep history of struggle, that we are here and now.

Jenna Lauter: *Transcendent.* These songs speak to universal truths that are able to transcend time and circumstance, and connect audiences from all walks of life.

Paola Mendoza: *Legacy.*

Nelini Stamp: *Power.* I want to build power for my community.

Ginny Suss: *Inspiring.* I look back to the civil rights movement and the labor movement, and so much of the singing was used to energize, to inspire people to keep fighting, to remind people of the inspiration that had brought them to these movements in the first place.

Arin Maya: *Strength.*

Sally Rumble: *Truth.*

Shaina Taub: *GROUNDBREAKING.* **gc**

CREATIVE BLOCK

ONE ILLUSTRATOR'S BIGGEST FEAR

BY SALLY NIXON

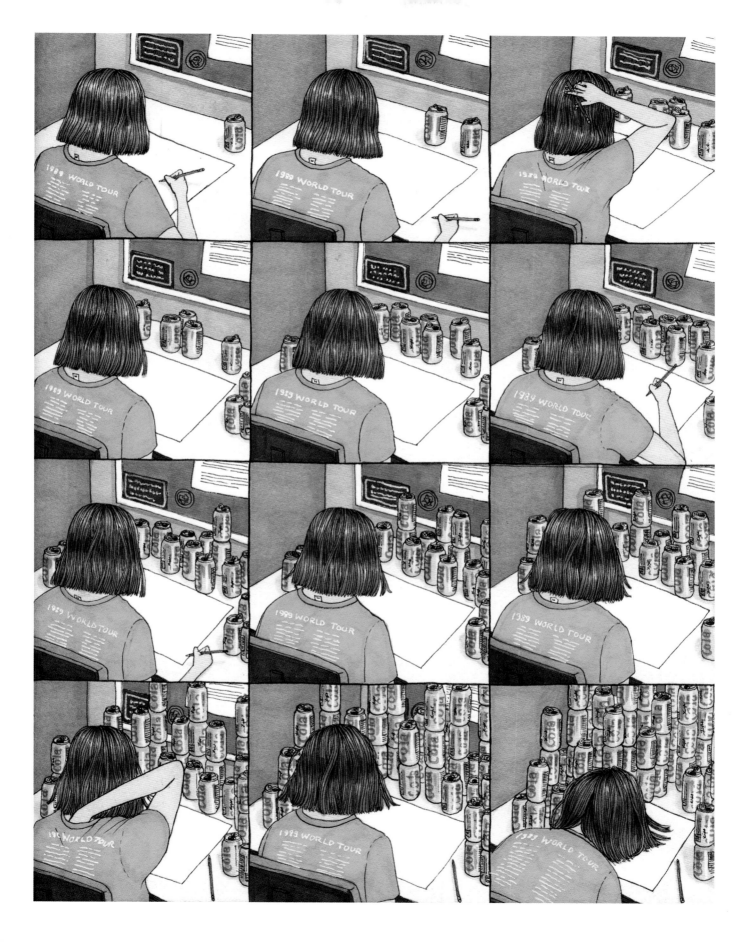

9 THINGS TO DO WHEN YOU DON'T KNOW WHAT TO DO.

Pet a dog.

Call a friend.

Meditate.

Read something.

Listen to something.

Watch something.

Clean.

Make a snack.

Go for a walk.

Even Africans Fall in Love

An Interview with film director Wanuri Kahiu   *By Kari Mugo*

Wanuri Kahiu's name now sits comfortably on the tongues of the likes of Ava DuVernay and Lupita Nyong'o following the premiere of Wanuri's feature film, *Rafiki*, at the 2018 Cannes Film Festival. *Rafiki* (meaning "friend" in Kiswahili) is herstory in the making as Kenya's first entry into the festival and adds Wanuri's name to the short list of women—eighty-two, to be precise—whose films have been screened at Cannes in its over seven-decade history.

The film, which premiered to a standing ovation, is banned for viewing or

Photo by Big World Cinema & AFROBUBBLEGUM

distribution in its home country. According to a statement released by the Kenya Film Classification Board (KFCB), the ban is a result of the film's "homosexual theme and clear intent to promote lesbianism in Kenya contrary to the law." *Rafiki* tells the story of two young girls from rival political families who fall in love. Kenya, like most African countries, continues to harass, discriminate against, and exact violence on sexual and gender minorities with the support of the state and fueled by homophobic rhetoric from its leaders and pulpits.

Wanuri's film runs contrary to popular morality by not only depicting same-sex love, but celebrating it. The KFCB took issue with this, asking Wanuri to change the film's ending to instead depict two remorseful young lovers. Wanuri declined. A ban ensued, adding *Rafiki* to a long history of censorship in Kenya that began in its colonial era and reached its peak during the twenty-six-year-long dictatorship of President Daniel arap Moi, when writers such as Ngũgĩ wa Thiong'o were forced into exile. More recently, Kenyan films like *Stories of Our Lives*, which features gay content, have been banned for viewing in Kenya.

I caught up with Wanuri as she was breathing in Cannes: Before the red carpets and the media blitz. Before anyone except her, the crew, and the KFCB had seen *Rafiki*. Under the hashtag #WaCannesDa, Wanuri and a bevy of African female creatives were preparing to make their mark on the festival with the all-too-rare story of two young Africans in love.

As the director, producer, and author tells me, the rarity of such stories was why she wanted to make a joyous love story. One that came to her in the form of the short story "Jambula Tree" by Monica Arac de Nyeko. Sweet, rich, and filled with longing, Arac de Nyeko's story won the Ugandan writer the 2007 Caine Prize for African Writing. It was on this footing that Wanuri and her crew undertook the task of fleshing out the world within "Jambula Tree," in the process moving the story from Uganda to the bubbly streets of Nairobi as imagined by a creator who believes in making "fun, fearless, and frivolous African art."

While *Rafiki* takes Wanuri one step closer to becoming a household name, for her, success, as defined by her own terms, remains on the horizon.

Let's start at the beginning. How did you get into film?

When I was sixteen, I knew I wanted to be a filmmaker. I walked into a space that was creating film and TV and I hadn't realized before that making films was an option. But once I realized that it was, I knew that was what I wanted to do.

You also cofounded a media company, AFROBUBBLEGUM. What is, and why, AFROBUBBLEGUM?

We've created a genre. AFROBUBBLEGUM is non-agenda-driven art. It's art driven by imagination, for art's sake. So often, out of Africa, a lot of the art we create is policy-driven. We don't have a chance to fully express ourselves. AFROBUBBLEGUM provides an outlet for artists to just be artists. Not having to try to seek funding for work that they have to do in order to advance a policy or agenda. It's fun, fearless, and frivolous African art. It is hopeful and joyful.

That's a really great point. I think a lot of the art Africans are expected to create needs to be hopeless, or there needs to be that "African struggle" in order for people to feel like it's authentic. Joyous African art sounds amazing. Having read "Jambula Tree," I'm curious: What spoke to you about that story?

My producer, Steven Markovitz, said he wanted to adapt modern African stories, so I started reading lots of stories. I really wanted to make a love story in particular, so I was reading lots of love stories. The story jumped off the page in such an amazing way. It was incredibly tender, it was kind. At the time, all the other love stories I was reading were a little hard. They weren't about the joys of love. This one really, really celebrated love.

There's a question around ownership that I'm struggling with as a queer woman when it comes to this story and your subsequent film. Here is a beautiful story about two women falling in love that is written by a self-described straight woman. Then taken on and produced by someone who, again, I assume is a straight woman. Did you struggle with whether this was your story to tell?

Love is love. Telling this story is about telling the story of young love and the

community's reaction to it. Because AFROBUBBLEGUM has become my genre, it's important to tell stories about the softness and kindness of Africans. I really wanted to make sure there's a space where we do that. Where we say, "You know, we have fun. We like to enjoy our lives, we fall in love," and that's why it was important for me to make this film. Also because, I don't know, when *did* you last see two young Africans in love on screen? I remember that the first time I did, I was way into my teens. I remember watching this couple and they were so cute and I was like, "Oh my gosh, even Africans fall in love!" It wasn't something that we saw often. But inevitably, that story was about the perils of HIV/AIDS. It wasn't just a story about being in love. It was reprimanding love.

I'm asking myself if I've ever seen a film with two Africans in love, and I'm disappointed to say that I can't recall this. Yet we consume so much Western media, we're constantly being given these representations of what love looks like, but what does love look like for us? Thank you for that.
What were some of your favorite parts of filming *Rafiki*?

The date scenes were absolutely some of my favorite! I've always wanted to go on a date in Uhuru Park [a public park and landmark adjacent to Nairobi's downtown area], so I made the girls go on a date in Uhuru Park because I haven't been. It was so much fun running around that park, riding the paddle boats and these really creaky rides. It was just awesome.

Samantha Mugatsia and Sheila Munyiva, the lead actresses, are so endearing in the movie trailer. I can also hear Muthoni Drummer Queen's (MDQ) song "Suzie Noma" playing in the background. That *Rafiki* is so strongly female-driven is one of the things that resonates with me.

We made a great soundtrack that is full of young African women. I'm super excited about the artists on the soundtrack. We have some of MDQ's work; we also have a young singer/songwriter known as Njoki Karu. Working on *Rafiki*, it's been really important for me to empower young women and that includes the musicians. The graphic designer who did the opening graphics is also a young woman. We felt it was important to pay attention and add value to the work other artists are doing.

To know that you were very conscious to cultivate this space is so empowering, so needed, so necessary.

That's why I feel like [Cannes this year] is about the celebration of young African women. So many young African women who are either film supporters or worked on the film are coming to Cannes to support the film. That's huge. We'll be a presence. There will be a female, African presence.

How did you feel when you found out about being accepted to this year's festival?

I was home when I found out. In the beginning, I was super incredulous. I was like, "Is there a letter? Where is the proof?" It's one of the biggest honors in the world to get into Cannes.

Do you feel like *Rafiki* is going to be one of the really big films out of Cannes?

Unfortunately and fortunately, the ban has put focus on the film. Unfortunately, it feels like the politics is coming before the art, and I really want the story and the film to stand out above all else. We made it to be seen, not debated by people who haven't watched it.

The members of the KFCB asked you to change the ending of the film and make other edits. It's interesting to me that individuals with no artistic background, who have never made a film or received recognition for any work in film, want to give you direction on how you should go about creating your own work. As a director, can you talk to me about that feeling?

It's the role of the audience to say all these things. It's their role to be able to say, "You shouldn't have done this, you could do this." But two things: One, the audience has the right to have that role, and two, to have that right, you have to have watched it. The people on the KFCB exercised their right to watch the film and make comments

based on having watched the film. The role of the artist is not necessarily to respond to every bit of feedback an audience gives.

That's very stoic of you. I'm so sensitive about my work.

People can speak. The moment that you release work, I feel, it no longer belongs to you.

There is a history in Kenyan art-making of content going into exile, which dates back to President Moi's era when Ngũgĩ wa Thiong'o and his peers were creating works of art that the government said no to. Their work had to go into exile. Do you feel like this particular film will go into exile, and what does that feel like?

I think the film goes into exile, I won't. I live in Kenya. I work in Kenya. My family is in Kenya. I have two children that I want to raise in Kenya, and I'm married in Kenya. It's my home and I don't plan to leave it, but the film will go into exile until the ban is rescinded.

Do you see that happening?

Ngũgĩ wa Thiongo's books came back. People are able to read them. The bans that existed during the Moi era were lifted on literature and theater, so perhaps?

I think it's inevitable that in our lifetimes we will be able to see these films . . .

In the country that they were made in.

There are a handful of Kenyan directors whom audiences know of, and to be a successful Kenyan female director and producer who has won awards and had her films recognized internationally is something that really stands out. What does that success feel like?

I think I'm working toward success. The good thing is, at some point in my life, I defined what success is for me and I'm still working toward that. I'm not there yet. But filmmaking is my job, it's my career in the same way accountants do their job. If they do their job well, they get accolades. So while those awards are great recognition of the hard work that not only myself but the cast and the crew have done, I don't necessarily see them as success. If that's

your definition of success, when you get an award, what next? What happens after that? Have you peaked? Have you then reached what you need to reach? What is your role after that? For me, success is more organic. It's more about the journey. Being a filmmaker for me is success, and continuing to be a filmmaker is success. **gc**

LUVVIE AJAYI

In the midst of a modern Black creative renaissance—and the resounding clapback of Trump and white tears—someone must rise up to bear the responsibility of conducting draggings and serving side-eye to the masses. Who better for the job than professional troublemaker and verbal virtuoso Luvvie Ajayi?

By Lindsey Day
Photography by Deun Ivory
Lettering by Erin Ellis

As a *New York Times* bestselling author, fifteen-year (award-winning) blogging veteran, speaker, and activist, it seems as though there isn't much Luvvie Ajayi *hasn't* accomplished. She was named on Oprah Winfrey's inaugural SuperSoul 100 list as someone who "elevates humanity," and has been honored by ADCOLOR, *Essence, Marie Claire, OkayAfrica,* and dozens of other esteemed platforms.

Her superpower? Breaking down complex, culturally sensitive topics into bite-size, digestible—if slightly salty—pieces. She doesn't mince words, and she *will* tell you about yourself. Yep, you too.

Whether dissecting the latest "Cheeto Satan" rant or pouring out her sentiments in posts like "About the Weary Weaponizing of White Women Tears" on her blog; chatting with faves like Jenifer Lewis and Myleik Teele about their lives and careers on her podcast, *Rants and Randomness*; or running the Red Pump Project, the HIV-education nonprofit she cofounded, she does it with heart and a huge dose of realness. For obvious reasons, I couldn't wait to talk to this dynamic woman about her mission, her process, and how she's learned to conquer her fears.

You're a woman of many titles, some self-proclaimed: Professional Troublemaker, Shady Nigerian, Supreme Side-Eye Artist . . . Who is Luvvie Ajayi? What is she on this earth to do?

Oh my gosh, that's such a good question. I am a writer and a truth-teller. And I think I've been placed on earth to bring joy, to make people think. Honestly, to change it a little bit. I have a gift of having people listen to big ideas in small bites and understanding it.

Tell me a bit about your early life. What brought your family to the US from Nigeria, and how did that move shape your upbringing?

I was born and raised in Nigeria and we came here [to Chicago] when I was nine. We had family here, we'd been here on vacation, and I think my mom just thought it was the right time. But we were culture-shocked, for sure. Going from where you are the default, in terms of what you look like, to being the new kid—all of the sudden your accent is strange, your name is strange, everything is strange. It's a shock to the system. But at nine, you're at the age of adapting, and I was able to adapt.

I actually listened to how my friends were speaking to learn how to lose my accent, and I lost it in a couple of years. When you're young, you don't want to stand out. That's not when you think being different is "cute." Essentially I was like, *Okay, how do I become less different? All right, your accent is different. Okay, so we begin to talk different.* I had lost most of my Nigerian accent by the time I started high school.

Was there a community or anything that helped give you a sense of place during this transition?

I mean at home, I was a fully Nigerian girl—Yoruba—eating Nigerian food, so I never lost touch with my culture or my sense of self in that way, because I had that. I think that was really kind of clutch. Just because we were here, doesn't mean all of the sudden you stop knowing where you come from or that you're no longer proud of who you are. And I think my mom also was an ever-present grounding force. African parents are the best grounding force, because no matter where you go or who you are, they can still check you at the drop of a hat.

I know that's right. What kind of student were you when you were young? Did you have any favorite subjects? Were you always a "writer"?

I was a really good student. I was the kid who would come home and do her homework immediately. I was always an A student. It was something that I kind of took pride in. I was a geek, I enjoyed school, I enjoyed writing. I didn't think, like, *Writing's my favorite subject.* But it probably was.

We might have been friends as kids—I was also a nerdy overachiever. [laughs] As a writer, you've become the person who "says what we might be thinking, but dare not to say." Is this just your natural personality, or were there any influences?

I really think it's my personality and my Nigerian-ness. People who know me will say that they hear my voice when they read my writing. And it's something that gives me joy because it shows that who I am shines through in my pen. I do think a huge part of my personality is in my writing because

Styling by Keri Henderson; makeup by Andrea C. Samuels

how I think, how I feel, or how I approach the world is essentially what makes up my writing. I think it's an innate gift.

For a long time, that's also why I didn't consider myself a writer. 'Cause I thought it was too easy. I thought, *Oh, I can't be a writer. Like, I'm not a novelist. Other people are novelists, other people are writers. I'm not Toni Morrison, I'm not J.K. Rowling. I'm just a girl who likes to talk about the things that she believes in and things that she's judging, or side-eying. That's not what a writer is!* So it took me a while to call myself a writer and to own it, because of that. And I think it's because, oftentimes, we tend to deny our gifts if they are too easy and don't come wrapped in struggle.

That's so real. I can really relate to that, as I know a lot of women can. Are there any women who have been important or influential in your life?

My mom, for sure. Just because of her selflessness—that's something she passed down to me. I just think she's a great person and woman. There's of course Oprah, 'cause I feel like every Black girl has looked to Oprah. She expanded our world, and expanded what we thought was possible for ourselves. She's somebody else who has insisted on living life on her own terms, insisted on being the person that she is—through all of it. That's admirable.

How, if at all, has their inspiration guided your voice?

I don't think about anybody else's voice but my own, because I think that's important.

You can admire people but you don't necessarily have to emulate them. Everybody's journey has to be theirs. So I don't really make it a point to try to write or do work like anybody else.

Tell me a little bit about your process as a writer. Do you ever experience writer's block? Or does it tend to flow because you're so heated about the subject matter?

My process is, I just sit down to write. Some people are like, "Oh my God, then I meditate . . ." I don't have all of that. I just . . . sit down and do the work. Put pen to paper and see what happens.

Any writer's block is more procrastination. I'm not writing because either I'm too busy, or because I'm not letting myself sit down long enough to be able to put my thoughts on paper. That's my version of writer's block. The times when I'm scatterbrained, I make an outline for exactly what I want to say and go off that. But I think most of the time it's just me being like, *Okay, there's this topic that I'm really caring about right now or feel compelled to write about, and so I'm going to sit down and put my thoughts down and see how they flow.* And then I do that. I go back, I edit, make my stream of consciousness more organized. I make sure that I'm saying what I mean. I get whatever else I want to say out, and then I post.

You started your blog in 2003 and were earning blogging awards in 2009, when some people—and major corporations—were still just starting to

catch on. You're an outlier. What set of circumstances or mind-set led you to blogging?

It wasn't something that I thought about as a career, it was just something that was like, *Oh, it's cute! I'll start a weblog.* And then it just took on a life of its own. Back then, a lot of people had blogs—like, online diaries. I just never stopped. So I just kept it going, and here I am.

How has your approach changed since then? How have you stayed current with new tools and just generally staying ahead of the curve?

I don't try to. I honestly just do what I do. I use different tools, but really, it's just the rules of communication. The rules of communication have not changed, really. I just stay true to my voice. I don't change my voice based on whatever platform I'm on. I'm not a different person based on where you land. I'm the same person across each one.

Do you have any pet peeves about people, like people's digital interactions now, or is there anything about the early days that you miss?

I have a lot of pet peeves about people right now. I think essentially the difference now is people start blogs to actually make money from them, and people start blogs with strategies. Back in 2003 and 2006 there wasn't none of that. You weren't blogging because you thought it was going to make you rich, you were blogging just

because you loved to write. So that's definitely something that has changed about content-creating. The OGs didn't have the expectations that people have now, and it allowed us to write in our best way possible. There wasn't the pressure of strategy and *How many page views are you going to get?* Naw, we didn't have any of that.

You're involved in vital—and viral—conversations that are important to the culture and carry a lot of weight. You've said in the past that just "Being yourself can be a revolutionary act." Does it get exhausting? Are there other voices or people in your life who you look to in those moments to feel like, "Okay, I'm not alone"?

My friends. I have a great group of friends who I can always compare notes with. When I'm having a rough day, they'll understand. I mean—I look less outwardly to, like, "the world" and more to what is actually surrounding me. I think it's important to curate people around us who we can look to and draw from. The people who matter the most in my life are those who I actually know. Less so the stars.

In the midst of the constant barrage of BS in the news/online, how do you decide who to "drag" or what conversation to sound off on?

I don't know if I have a grand strategy. Honestly, it depends on the day. There's some topics that I am compelled to write about that I just don't end up having time to write about, if I'm traveling that day or I

have deadlines looming; and then there are some days when I'm actually home when I'm able to write, and I'm like, *Great, I can put pen to paper.*

Sometimes I won't have time to write about something in the moment, and my audience will let me know, "Hey, we're looking for your voice on this." And I'll be like, "Oh great. Y'all actually want to hear about this topic? I didn't have time last week but I have time now if you still want to hear about it." I honestly just write the things that I'm compelled to write. I usually can't be forced to write about something.

The internet is so massive, the conversations could go on forever— and to be frank, people can be assholes. How do you process things privately and make sure you're pouring into yourself so you can pour back out into us/them culture?

I take social media breaks. I don't typically announce them or anything, but I like, won't be on the internet for like a week. To just kinda get my brain back, to stop some of the information overload. And to quiet my mind a little bit, because I think you get so much input online, and you end up not being at peace because you're constantly hearing. Things being thrown at you. So yeah, I take breaks. I take naps, I go on vacation. I have day-long sabbaticals where I'm just off the grid, just enjoying life without the internet. I think that's important.

Sometimes entrepreneurship is glamorized. The whole "be your own boss, follow your dreams" thing. What

are your thoughts on that, and do you have any big sister advice for people looking to take the plunge?

The grass is always greener on the other side. I know sometimes I'm envious of people who can leave work at five p.m. and not have to touch it again until nine a.m. the next day.

There's many days where I'm like, *Dang, I miss being able to* not *work.* You really don't stop working as an entrepreneur. It's one of these weird things. There are times when I am in my head like, *Shoot, I didn't reply to that email. Ah, I need to finish this media kit.* It never turns off.

I always tell people that doing work for yourself is not just about the carefree, "I'm gonna run after my dreams" thing. You can actually take a leap of faith by first building your net. If you know you want to work for yourself, you don't have to quit your job today and just be *out here.* You can know, "I want to work for myself," spend a year planning it and stacking *all* your coins— 'cause you're going to need *all* the coins— and then plan your exit as opposed to how some people just expect to go out in a blaze of glory: "I quit!" No, that's not realistic, especially if you're a parent or you're somebody that other people depend on for their survival. You can't just be up and quitting if you don't have a nest egg. Of course, if you got laid off your job all of the sudden, that's one thing, but otherwise, you can actually plan out the best way.

Or that leap can get real short, real quick.

Correct. People romanticize entrepreneurship, especially recently. I've been seeing a

lot of it. People just being like, "Hey, you should just be following your dreams," or "Every moment you are working for somebody else, you're helping somebody else build their dreams." Some people don't *have* the dream of working for themselves, and that's perfectly fine. I don't think we should be romanticizing it. We have to be clear that our dreams are not everybody else's dreams. And that's perfectly fine. You don't have to all have the same dream. We don't all have to think that our lives are what everybody should aspire to. My whole goal is to also let people know that, like, "Here's the wheel, you make the decision that works for you now."

Today, you're a *New York Times* bestselling author, for *I'm Judging You: The Do-Better Manual.* Can you talk about the shift in mind-set from, "I'm not really a writer" to "Oh shit, I'm a bestselling author!"?

Eventually, I had to admit to myself that I am a writer. Kind of like, *You've been doing this thing for a long time. And, yeah, you actually are gifted at it.* Just because you don't struggle at it doesn't mean you can't claim it.

I got the idea for my book in 2014. And I knew that, of course, I wanted to first and foremost create something that I was really proud of. And then I was like, *I want to be a* New York Times *bestselling author!* And saying that out loud, and asking people to help me see it come true—that was really important, because sometimes we think things are so far-fetched that we don't even dream them. But I was like, *I'm going to wish for this thing to happen.* And when it happened—when my book came out September 13, 2016—it actually hit the *Times*'s list that week. Instantly. So it felt amazing. It felt amazing. I was just like, *Woooow*. So it *is* possible for us to see our dreams come true.

That's bananas. It was surreal, but it was also like, *All right, I worked for this. And this is something that I deserve and I've earned.* So making it a point to not question our work and our value when we see these things come true is so important.

As an entrepreneur you can take a lot of L's before you get those wins, so I can imagine it must have just been a major shift. Did this win help with the "impostor syndrome"? Or is it not that simple?

Well, it's one of those moments where it's like, I'm in an elite club now. I've absolutely earned my place in certain rooms. If you want to be really logical about it, you are now in a category that most people will never be in, so you will find yourself in rooms that most people will never be in. I thought that it was also important to share all of the journey, and to talk about it. *I'm here, but it isn't by happenstance. Here's the work that brought me into this room.* Because I didn't want people who saw my journey to randomly think I was just, like, showing up places without earning it. So I was being very diligent about telling people about the stories. What were the processes that had to happen for me to be in this place?

We would talk ourselves out of everything if we let ourselves. But there's no

honor in that. I think women, especially, have been told that being humble to a fault is okay. We've been told not to be confident. We've been told that things sound braggadocious. No, no. Being able to say, "I'm a *New York Times* bestselling author, that's why I can command certain fees, that's why I can be in these rooms . . ." isn't bragging, it just is.

Coming from the digital space, how did it feel to see a product you've worked on become a real, tangible thing, going out into the world and I'm sure blowing up your social media? What was that like for you?

I mean, it felt great. It's humbling to see this thing that you worked on come to life. And to hold it in your hands makes it even more real. When you finish your manuscript and you're like, *Okay, the final period is here*, the work is just really starting. You still have to edit, you still have to do all these things. So when you see it finally printed, it's like . . . *Oooooh. Okay. This thing that I did, it's not just a concept anymore, it's a* thing. *It's alive, it's here. I can share it with the world.* It felt amazing.

What scares you most? What major fear(s) have you had to push through to get to this place?

Honestly, the unknown. Again, I had to push through the whole writing thing. And working for yourself is the unknown because you're used to getting guaranteed checks. You had a boss who told you what to do. Now it's, *I am the boss, I am the*

bringer of everything. If I don't work, I don't *eat.* And that's a scary prospect, because it puts the onus of everything on you.

But like with everything, you have to push past it if it's worth doing. People think about the word *fearless* to mean "without fear," but I see it to actually mean "with fear, but you did it anyway." I don't think anybody is fearless; without any type of fear, or any type of thing that makes them pause—without any type of thing that intimidates them. I think the difference is, there are some people who are afraid, but who are more committed to insisting that they're not going to let the fear be what stops them.

It's a practice. There will never be a time where there's all of the sudden three steps to take that'll make you stop being afraid of doing something. It just comes down to committing to push back in that moment when you're like, "I shouldn't do it." You just have to swallow it down and say, "I'm gonna do it anyway." It's like when you're going into a pool and the water's really cold. You just have to step into it and just have that moment when you gasp. It's the same thing. Like, you can dip your toe into it. Sure. And then you dip your second toe. Sure, that helps. It takes a little bit longer. Or you can just jump right into it. **gc**

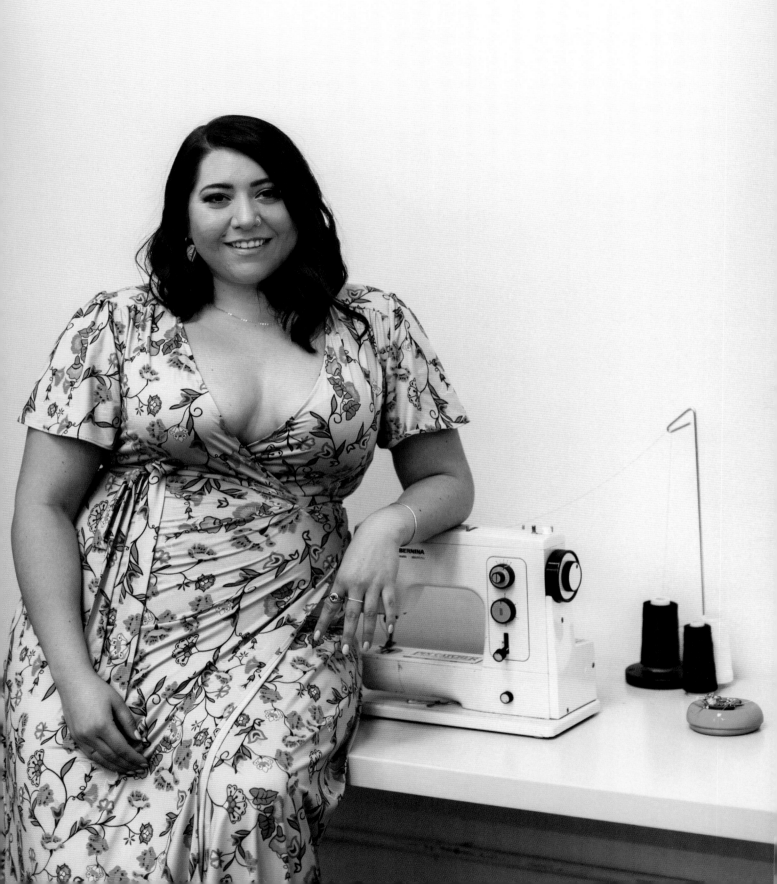

The Rise and Bloom of Bethany Yellowtail

Fashion designer Bethany Yellowtail discusses why her mission always involves supporting the voices and work of her community.

By Kelli Hart Kehler
Photography by Caroline Ingraham Lee

About twelve years ago, on the Crow Indian Reservation in southeastern Montana, a high school–aged Bethany Yellowtail wanted out. Surrounded for miles and miles by land, she'd lived her whole life on the reservation, carving a space for herself where she didn't see one. She stood in stark contrast to her peers dressed in Wranglers, cowboy boots, T-shirts, and cowboy bling—"I'd make my own Pendleton jackets and wear Baby Phat, it was kind of like indigenous hip-hoppy," Bethany remembers. "Like Jenny from the block meets the rez. That was me, and I really had my own unique, individual style, and I just didn't fit in."

Despite living among her own suppor- tive reservation community outside of school hours—her heritage belonging to both Apsáalooke (Crow) and Tsetsehesta- hese & So'taeo'o (Northern Cheyenne) tribes—Bethany attended school in a bor- der town between Montana and Wyoming, and racism was pervasive in her educational surroundings.

"I was one of maybe five Native kids

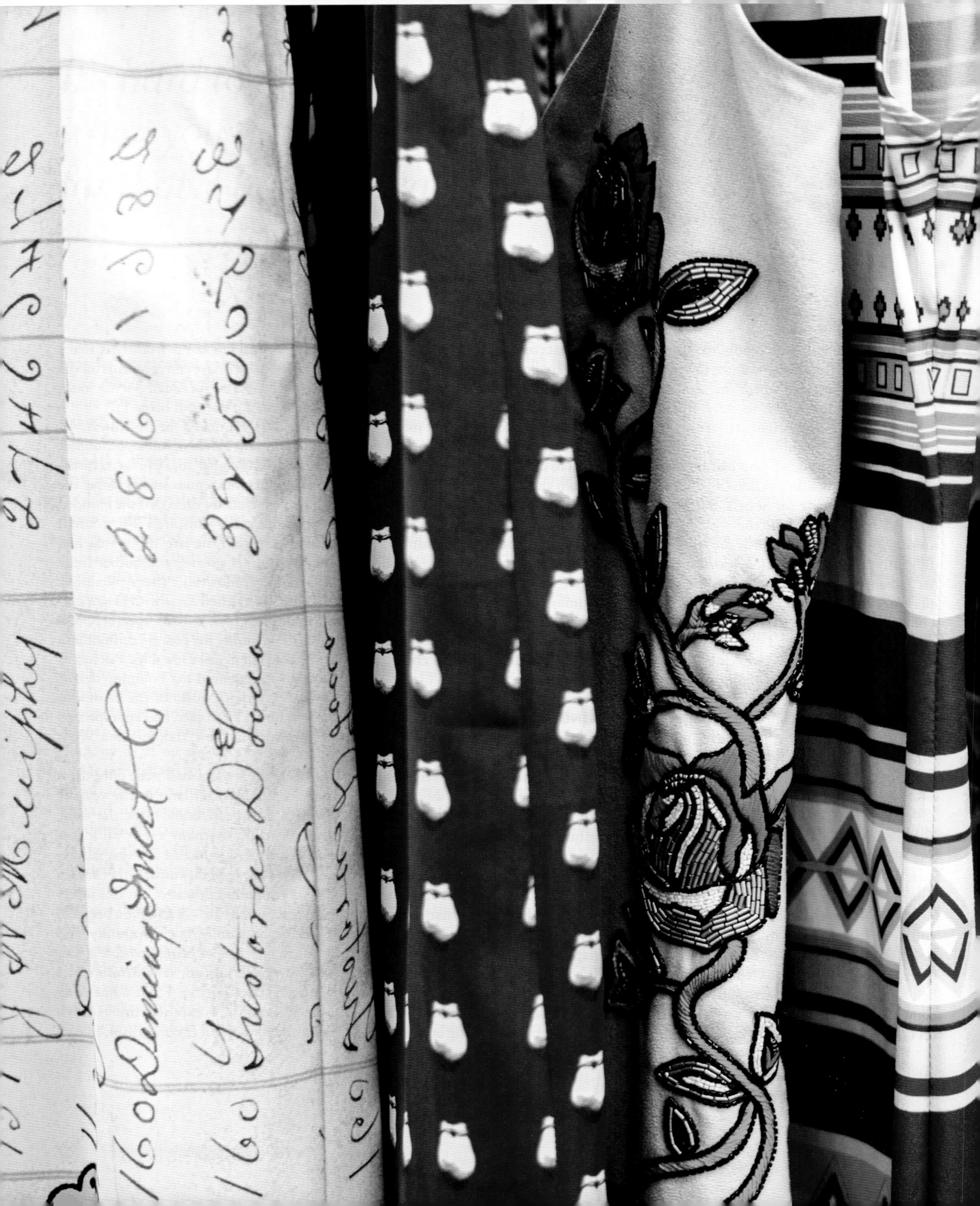

> *I had to "cowboy up" to figure out how to do things with what I had. But that's also what our people have always done. We make beautiful things with not a whole lot.*

tendency for a lot of Native people—if we put ourselves out there, it's just going to get taken from us."

Cultural appropriation and representation are inherently intertwined ideals, with one informing the other in a cyclical pattern: Sometimes more representation emerges in response to cultural appropriation, and sometimes, like in Bethany's experience, representation can spur cultural appropriation. In any case, Bethany understands that continued representation is worth the risk of appropriation that follows, as the more indigenous stories are told and shared, the more they're understood as an important part of both history and modern society. "In all ways, Native people have had to battle that," she says. "It's the twenty-first century and we're still combating those erasures."

PUTTING TOGETHER THE PIECES
Throughout Bethany's time in Los Angeles building her entrepreneurial career, she's had moments that have energized and re-affirmed her, blooming her spirit even in the face of the racism and stereotypes she's experienced against her Native community. At the end of 2016, she felt a strong energy pulling her to Standing Rock, where many tribes were gathering in solidarity to stand up against the Dakota Access Pipeline. One of her friends posted a photo of herself on Facebook, set up under an awning with a single sewing machine, attempting to sew as many ribbon skirts as she could in order

to properly dress women at the camp so they could participate in a prayer ceremony.

"When I saw those things going on at Standing Rock, I knew that I needed to go and go with purpose, not just take up space," Bethany reflects. "I wanted to help dress people, because those are important roles in our community, so I got together supplies and took out hundreds of yards of wool fabric, and we got five or six sewing machines and generators—all the supplies we needed to have a sewing base camp. And I went out to go teach people how to sew and do a workshop on how to make ribbon skirts with some of the women who were already out there so we could facilitate space."

With fashion and creativity embedding themselves into her life from her earliest memories, and the people along the way who've recognized and championed her raw talents and passion, it was not until this time at Standing Rock that Bethany connected the pieces of how fashion was meant to inform her life. "I had this moment where I was looking around and there were tepees up and people riding on horseback, there were people chopping wood and tending fires and painting people, and I was just like, 'Wow, this is literally what I was always meant to do. Here I am, back in our homelands,' because actually where we were on the river was the same place that my ancestors had been at one certain time—the Cheyenne people lived along the Missouri near there, so that is actually part of my ancestral homelands before we got

to where we are now in Montana. I literally felt my ancestors calling me to be there and contribute. Our people always had roles for each individual, and I know I stepped into mine, and it looks different now than it did before. It's still a continuity of the way our tribal communities operate. It was a moment of clarity for me, and it gave me another boost to just keep moving forward."

NOT ACTIVISM
In a time when activism is en vogue and everyone is more inspired to join a march or stand up for a cause than they have been in recent years, the fashion industry is becoming saturated with political messages and calls to action. But Bethany's role in integrating indigenous representation and fashion isn't something she happened upon overnight—it's in her blood.

"I still don't really call myself an activist," she begins. "The way I look at it is, I'm an indigenous woman and I understand my responsibility. That's the way I see myself." Bethany took her recent epiphany from her observations at Standing Rock and put it to work on another platform where she could successfully amplify Native representation: the inaugural Women's March on Washington in January 2017. She designed the Indigenous Women Rise scarf, a turquoise silk scarf emblazoned with a Woman Warrior emblem, to honor Native women who came before and inspire the next generation to rise up.

"I still can't get the image out of my

THE MOVEMENT OF MOVEMENTS RETURNS INDIGENOUS VOICES TO THE FOREFRONT AND AMPLIFIES THE INTERCONNECTEDNESS OF ALL BEINGS. IN ACCORDANCE WITH NATURAL LAW, WE'VE ANSWERED THE CALL TO STAND UP AND RISE.

WE ARE THE RESILIENT

People get to see that Native people and indigenous women are more complex and have more to offer than just the stereotypical imagery that [is] out there.

head of when I was at the Women's March and there were a thousand Native women and allies wearing my bandannas and scarf that had the Women Warrior design on it—it united us. And when we walked through the march, the seas parted and people recognized that indigenous people are still here in a very, very powerful way, and it was because of the design that I had created that united us. And I'll always remember that."

ALTER-NATIVE

In the summer of 2016, Bethany was approached by Native filmmaker Billy Luther to showcase her work and life in a documentary. Bethany's activism—or "responsibility," as she prefers to define it—was also chronicled in *alter-NATIVE*, a six-part docuseries journaling a year in her life. The first episode of the series opens with Bethany enveloped in her fashion design work and freshly adjusting from a major breakup. As someone who thrives on being behind the scenes, she was hesitant to open herself up in such a vulnerable way, to have her personal life on display, but Bethany trusted Billy and his understanding of her life through a Native lens. "The bigger picture is that this contemporary story, which happens to be mine, gets to be told, and people get to see that Native people and indigenous women are more complex and have more to offer than just the stereotypical imagery and the stereotypical stories that are out there."

THE NEXT GENERATION

As Bethany has worked throughout her life to carve out space for her to exist and be seen as an indigenous woman in contemporary America, she has, in turn, become an example for the next generation of Native youth. Where she struggled to find anyone to look up to in mainstream media or fashion as a teen, she now serves as a beacon of representation and success for others. And she's emboldened to take on cultural appropriation and help get her community the respect it rightfully deserves.

"[Most people] don't really think of us as contemporary people—we're still just fighting for humanity and visibility. That really resonates with me because I have family members who sell leather goods or beadwork or jewelry just to keep the lights on or to feed their families or to get gas to make it through the week. I imagine, what if our people didn't have to combat cultural appropriation, what if we had ownership of our own cultural identity through art and through our own goods and we were able to create an economy and that wasn't taken away from us? Because it's such a huge industry, specifically fashion—a billion-dollar industry. I don't know if you could name a single designer that hasn't used indigenous influence. But that literally takes away from our livelihood, and it takes away from our creative identity."

Her family, while supportive and proud of her fashion career, have fears that her political activism will hurt her business. "My dad, his father . . . grew up in a time where there were still signs on local storefronts that said 'No dogs or Indians allowed.' There's still these really real fears and persecutions that they experienced in their generations. So I understand why they feel that way," Bethany shares.

But since *alter-NATIVE* aired, Bethany says, her parents have a better understanding of the way her fashion and activism intertwine—the way they've always been closely woven together. "The people that support our business, they know that this is what we stand for," she says. "This is what contemporary Native America looks like, and I want people and allies to understand that. With the work we do, we're able to use fashion as a catalyst for these messages—that's the most surprising thing about where life has taken me." **gc**

The B. Yellowtail Collective

After Bethany launched her business, she returned home for three months to plan her next collection. While visiting the only gas station on the reservation, a man approached her while she was waiting in line to pay and asked her if she'd like to buy a pair of earrings he'd made. "At the time I didn't know this would be another lightbulb, life-changing moment," she remembers. The man had priced the intricate jewelry at $15 so he could buy gas for the week.

Bethany's heart sank—with her knowledge of material cost and labor, she knew the earrings were worth at least $100. She wanted to do more to amplify the work and skills of indigenous makers, so in 2016 she launched the B. Yellowtail Collective, a platform for sharing and selling the handmade work of Native American artisans and creating a "force of creative indigenous energy." Now the works of artists from tribes all over North America are elevated to a market where

they're priced appropriately and seen by a farther-reaching customer base.

"There's so much more out there," Bethany says, adding that this step is just the beginning of how she'd like to help strengthen the workforce of her Native community. "This is a small sampling of what Indian country really has to offer. They jumped in with me and it's been such a joy to celebrate with many different artists and community members."

ANDREA PRESTON
NAVAJO

Describe what you make:

I create art/jewelry that is inspired by the tradition of Navajo weaving geometrics and the influences of powwow culture. I use multimedia to integrate traditional imagery with modern contemporary design concepts. For the B. Yellowtail Collection, I create specific beaded jewelry and accessories. I'd like to think that my work speaks of truth and healing that stems from my own personal journey as a contemporary indigenous woman.

I really try to "lean into" the uncomfortable when it comes to obstacles in my life, not in a way where I'm in danger of course, but in ways that I am face-to-face with the things that make me uncomfortable. I lean into it until it's no longer something that is uncomfortable or limiting. It's not always easy to be brave when leaning into that uncomfortableness, though, and for those moments, I lean on the strong women in my life and I create art. I've been blessed with a handful of strong women, including Bethany, who support me and hold me up when I need to feel brave for life. And art—it's always been medicine. It has helped me in more ways than one.

ALAYNEE GOODWILL
LAKOTA/DAKOTA SIOUX

Describe what you make:

I create contemporary accessories using traditional materials and artistic practices.

How do you find strength when you face fear in either your personal life or creative work?

I was diagnosed with SLE (systemic lupus erythematosus) in 2014, and it completely changed my life. I struggled a lot the first two years. It wasn't easy coming to terms with limitations and fear of the unknown. I worked a lot on my mental health and found a lot of strength in just believing in myself and using the tools I already had in knowing what is best for my life.

JAYMIE CAMPBELL
MISSISSAUGA OJIBWE, CURVE LAKE
FIRST NATION, ANISHINAABE

Describe what you make:

My work is inspired by my Anishinaabe heritage, but also influenced by the time I've spent with the Cree people of the Rocky Mountains and the Dene of the north. I owe great gratitude to the Cree elders who have taught and continue to teach the old ways, which inspire much of my work. I want to inspire young people to know you can be athletic and artsy, scientific and spiritual, a warrior and an artist. White Otter Co. strives to use authentic materials in all of the work, and you will often see the use of hand-tanned hides, horsehair, and porcupine quills. Much of the material is sourced from local communities and elders, though I put a strong focus on learning the traditional skills in order to use them in my work and pass them down to future generations. I focus much of my work on traditional moccasins and wraparounds, framed beadwork, jewelry. and beaded smudge feather wraps.

When I face fear in my personal or creative life, I find strength in my family and my ancestors. I often feel my grandmothers around me, which lends me the strength they all collectively hold to be strong Anishinaabe women. My parents, siblings, and husband are all supportive and encourage me along my path personally and in creative fulfillment. Spending time on the land also always renews my spirit and grounds me in Mother Earth.

JAIDA GREY EAGLE
OGLALA LAKOTA

Describe what you make:

I make long, beaded fringe earrings that are unique by the gradient colors. I use size 13 charlotte-cut beads that make them light on the ears to wear. I love big earrings but cannot wear heavy earrings, so I found my way around that by using tiny beads. I intermix precious metal beads with contemporary and vintage beads. Each pair is unique in that I use so many colors, it's hard to re-create the same pair.

How do you find strength when you face fear in either your personal life or creative work?

I find strength in all walks of life in a note my late mother left us. She wrote, "Never give up! Fully live in this big beautiful world and do not limit yourself. Always believe you can truly do anything you want. I did."

JENNIFER YOUNGER
TLINGIT EAGLE/BEAR,
KAAGWAANTAAN

Describe what you make:

Contemporary engraved copper and silver jewelry, with Tlingit formline design, floral patterns, and spruce root basket patterns. I occasionally incorporate antique trade beads and spruce roots into my pieces.

How do you find strength when you face fear in either your personal life or creative work?

Having an element of fear does motivate me to work harder at what I do. Some of my fears are: Can I continue to support myself and my family doing this art form? Will this be enough to help carry the Tlingit art of formline to the next generations? Will people like and accept what I am creating? I don't want to offend my elders or anyone, for that matter. There are times that the fear and worry start to creep in, over circumstances or a decision. That's when I remind myself that everything happens for a reason that may not yet be apparent, and that I need to have faith and be patient. Surrounding yourself with people who uplift and support you is also huge. I've had the good with the bad. I choose to focus on the positive while dealing with the negative.

DEBORAH MAGEE SHERER
PIIKANI NATION (BLACKFEET)

Describe what you make:

I use my ancestors' medium of porcupine quillwork in my creative work. Quillwork is an ancient art medium among North American Native tribes that was and still is considered a sacred art among many.

In my tribe, one must go through the proper protocols and be given the rights by an elder or another quillworker to do quillwork. There are protocols for gathering and harvesting the quills, always with respect for the animal. Quillworkers are to be peaceful, well-grounded people; if you have lots of chaos and conflict in your life, it will be reflected in your quillwork. Therefore, quillwork teaches us how to live as *nit-si-tapi*, or "real people."

How do you find strength when you face fear in either your personal life or creative work?

Fear is a deadly, paralyzing emotion that keeps us from going forward in our creative, as well as personal, life. It keeps us from reaching our creative potential and hinders our creative exploration and growth. I deal with fear by analyzing it, taking it apart piece by piece, and naming each fear. I offer it to my God and ask for it to be taken away. If it doesn't change the emotion, then I have to let go of whatever was the cause of that fear, be it an art show, a toxic person, or even a piece I'm working on. Then it loses its power over me and blows away with the chinook winds.

CATHERINE BLACKBURN
DENE (ENGLISH RIVER FIRST NATION)

Describe what you make:

Inspired by the northern floral and geometric designs of my Dene roots, my handmade jewelry is a fusion of traditional and contemporary. My indigenous-made collections bring together rich color and culture to form luxurious, wearable art. Blurring the lines between everyday wear and bold signature pieces, this dynamic collection exudes edgy glamour and timeless northern design in jewelry that is both refined and functional.

How do you find strength when you face fear in either your personal life or creative work?

In two ways: I either throw myself into work, or I break completely from it and focus on my mental health by stepping away from the studio. I have a tremendously supportive family and group of friends, so no matter the distance between us, a phone call or visit seems to remedy whatever indecision, fear, anxiety, or stress I'm dealing with at the moment. If I throw myself into work, it is beadwork. Beading is a healing medicine, and through focus and reflection I can slow everything down and recharge.

MAYA STEWART
CHICKASAW, CHOCTAW, MUSCOGEE (CREEK)

Describe what you make:

I make accessible fashion accessories and handbags with high-quality materials from Italy and Japan, and inspired by my Native American heritage and rock 'n' roll.

How do you find strength when you face fear in either your personal life or creative work?

I find strength by focusing on positive energy in my surroundings and beauty in even the smallest things in my life.

GEO NEPTUNE
PESKOTOMUHKATI (PASSAMAQUODDY)

Describe what you make:

I gather and prepare black ash and sweet grass to make contemporary versions of traditional Passamaquoddy baskets, and incorporate glass and metal beads as well as semiprecious gems into my wearable woven art.

How do you find strength when you face fear in either your personal life or creative work?

When I face fear in my personal life, it reflects in my creative work, and I find strength by taking the traditions that have been handed down to me and adding my own spirit to them. I think that in order to survive, indigenous peoples have constantly had to adapt and evolve our traditions, and our art is a physical representation of that; I find strength in knowing that by making baskets, our stories will be accessible to future generations, and Two-Spirit youth will not feel as alone as I once did.

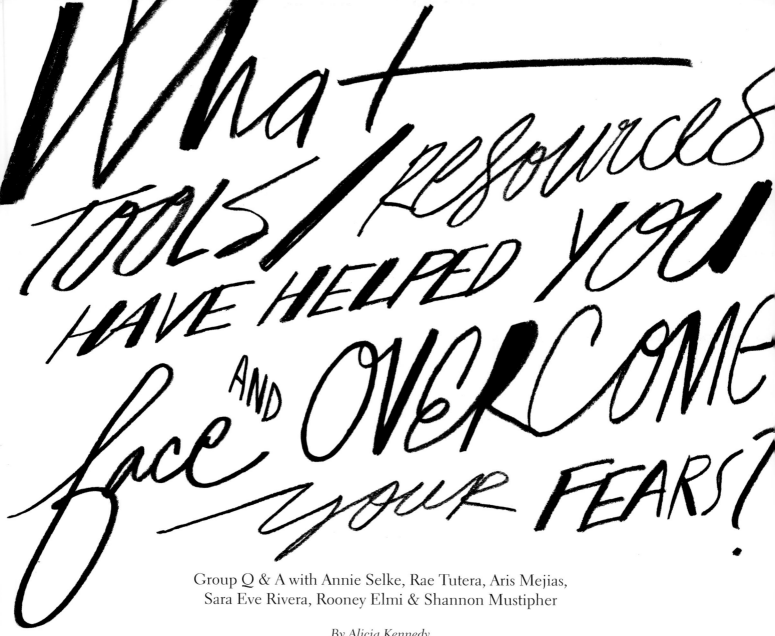

What TOOLS / RESOURCES HAVE HELPED YOU face AND OVERCOME your FEARS?

Group Q & A with Annie Selke, Rae Tutera, Aris Mejias,
Sara Eve Rivera, Rooney Elmi & Shannon Mustipher

By Alicia Kennedy
Illustration by Lauren Tamaki

We creative professionals are pushed to be bold and fearless in all aspects of our lives. To be capable of demanding our worth, comfortable making connections, and courageous in pursuit of our goals are matters of survival. But that takes practice.

To get perspective on how to cope with fear, I spoke to Annie Selke, home goods designer; Rae Tutera, clothier at Bindle & Keep and co-owner of Willoughby General; Aris Meijias, actor and designer of Skin Onion; Sara Eve Rivera, tattoo artist and owner of PMA Tattoo; Rooney Elmi, film critic and founder of *SVLLY(wood)*; and Shannon Mustipher, rum expert and bartender. From gazing at nature to trusting mentors, here's how they choose to deal with the fear inherent to being human.

What are your biggest fears, either in life or work?

Rae Tutera: My biggest fear is a specific form of failure: I'm afraid of failing folks, whether they're a part of my life or a part of

69

my work (or both, because there's often an overlap). I'm not afraid of failing at things—I'm almost eager to fail because I know that it will lead to growth. But I *am* afraid of failing others.

Aris Mejias: I think my personal biggest fear is being alone. Not solitude, which represents the capacity of being alone as a choice, but being alone by abandonment. Ironically, this fear used to make me a solitary being. I still float between reaching out to and shying away from people.

Sara Eve Rivera: My largest fear used to be that I would never get to learn how to tattoo. In tattooing, there is a historical standard that women are expected to date in, marry in, or at the very least be sexually available to male tattooers in order to learn how to tattoo. This standard still exists in different forms to this day. My greatest fear was that this standard would hold me back, that I would never get to tattoo full-time at a shop, but I couldn't picture doing anything else with my life.

Rooney Elmi: There was a time when failure was my biggest fear, but now I welcome it. I'm not the type to have beginner's luck, so failure tends to be the first step on my personal path to trying something new. I would've felt crippling fear hosting a party or shooting a film just a couple of years ago, but now I'm doing both. Fear is merely an obstacle to achieving my goals; I refuse to let it paralyze me again.

Shannon Mustipher: My biggest fear is of not having or being "enough"—while there are a variety of forms this can take, it all comes down to a fear of lack. Do I have the time, the energy, the money, etc., to get this thing done, or to attain this goal? I have found that most of my fears have their origins here. The challenge is to be honest about it and to open myself up to having faith that there is a way, in spite of how things might appear in that moment. The next step is to move forward, trusting that even if that thing doesn't come to pass in the way I originally envisioned it, I can be open to accepting that what came about instead is actually better suited to me and what I need in that moment or at that time.

What are the ways in which fear inspires or motivates you?

Annie Selke: The fear of failure keeps me working pretty diligently at pretty much any task, whether it's cooking a meal at home or creating a product or growing my business. I am a chronic overdeliverer!

Rae Tutera: Fear often manifests itself as curiosity for me. That might be because I'm an Aries—the baby of the chart, which means I can be impulsive. Acting on a fear as fast as possible has been an aggressive way of giving fear less space to occupy in my mind. That's the potentially unhealthy way fear has motivated me. The healthier way fear motivates me is because I'm hell-bent on not failing others. My fear of failing them inspires me to be as accountable as possible to all the folks I know in my life and in my work.

Aris Mejias: The fear of being alone really resonates with me. It has made me recognize I am a social being. I used to be very shy, and now I recognize freely that I love meeting people, and knowing their stories and thoughts. Sharing is a big part of my everyday life (not social media sharing, but actual communication between friends and family).

Sara Eve Rivera: The things I fear motivate me to work the long hours required to grow as a shop owner and tattooer alike. The skills I learned at the front desk really helped me to focus on client collaborations as well as cover-up tattooing. It pushed me to prove wrong those who told me tattooing was not possible, people who told me that the place for women in tattooing was "on the cover of tattoo magazines, not inside of them." Through that hard work, as well as studying the front-of-house work that many other tattooers do not experience, I became centrally focused on the concept of collaboration, reclamation, and empowerment tattooing. And now here we are, in a magazine!

Rooney Elmi: Fear is such a raw, visceral emotion that can be translated in so many ways that could be chaotic or rewarding depending on the avenue you choose to take. Personally speaking, converting fear into my creativity is both inspiring and motivating. I feel like I tend to dabble in themes of horror (specifically surveillance) in my work, so it makes much more sense that way.

Shannon Mustipher: Fear motivates me to get curious about the need or desire that needs attention. From there, it's time to get creative and start looking for ways to create the end result that I want.

Describe a time you overcame fear, creatively or professionally.

Annie Selke: There are, of course, many micromoments of fear—the call you really don't want to make, the tackling of a new topic or process—but what gives me sleepless nights is public speaking! When I do actually commit to a speaking engagement—and trust me, it's rare—it turns me inside out. Everyone thinks that because I am an inherently gregarious person, there is nothing I would get a kick out of more than addressing a crowd of a hundred to three hundred people! So when I do get through a speech and the crowd is happy with what they came to hear, I feel a particularly poignant sense of relief.

Rae Tutera: When I first began my apprenticeship with Bindle & Keep, I was responsible for building my queer clientele from scratch. It was exciting to let folks know about the work I was trying to do, but the reality was when those queer clients did

show up for fittings, both Daniel Friedman (founder of Bindle & Keep and my mentor) and I were only just learning how to do the work. I was learning to measure, and Daniel was learning how to be an ally in this context. Our clients trusted us with their bodies and their stories. Their bodies and their stories are what empowered us to fuse our talents. It was a risk for everyone involved. I was only really able to overcome my fear because I really believed in providing accessible and affirming service to my community. I knew it could and had to be done. When I couldn't trust myself, I trusted Daniel. I trusted our clients. I trusted some more evolved, generous version of myself. Answering these questions has reminded me how relationship-oriented I am, how much I relish collaboration, and how important mentorship has been for my growth.

Aris Mejias: I do not think I have overcome my fears at all. They are definitely part of who I am. So far, both of my career choices (actor and clothing designer) have helped to manage these waters. Acting has given me tools for self-analysis through characters, and sewing/designing for my clothing brand has given me enough solitude to think while working. Both acting and sewing will always provide something that I will proudly share with the world and that gives me purpose.

Sara Eve Rivera: I slowly overcame this fear and anxiety by working my way into the tattoo community. My experience as a tattoo

artist independently, outside of apprenticeship, was a powerful experience. For the first time, I had the freedom to come into my own as an artist through developing my own approach and style. I found my own voice and learned about tattoo shops and tattooing through some positive as well as negative experiences.

Rooney Elmi: Without going into too much detail, I think leaving a certain job position was the scariest thing I've done. It was an amalgamation of trusting my gut instinct and knowing it was the right time to leave. I fully believe that when it's most scary to jump, that's when you jump, or you remain stagnant forever.

Shannon Mustipher: Writing my first book—I had anxiety around whether what I had to say would make a meaningful impact. I realized that the best thing I could do was to keep it simple and focus on the things that inspired me to create cocktails, and trust that it would find its way to the people who would appreciate and enjoy it.

What tools or support systems have you used to overcome or better understand fear?

Rae Tutera: I have a habit of saying yes to things that stir up fear in me. Public speaking used to be one of my worst fears, and I can't say that I'm not afraid of it now, but I have said yes to enough invitations to speak in public to make them lose their visceral impact. So one of my tools is immersion.

Aris Mejias: My utmost important tool for dealing with fears is nature and its chaotic order. I will crave to sit in front of a plant, look at the sky and birds or ants. It gives me focus and it is truly my spiritual outlet. I have many plants in my living spaces, and I will always strive to be surprised by the unexpected. It is undeniably who I am.

Sara Eve Rivera: My clients have been the best support system this gal could ask for. Their trust, encouragement, and kindness have motivated me to keep growing as an artist and a human being. They present me with very exciting and unique tattoo concepts to develop into final designs. The adjustments that they ask me to make to designs encourage me to think creatively in the moment and keep my design skills sharp. I learn a lot from talking to them about their lives and personal experiences.

Shannon Mustipher: Journaling is the one that I go to most often. I can do it anytime, anywhere. I can do it with a pen and paper (my favorite medium), or tap it out on my phone. I've found that fear closely ties to the unknown—our reptilian brains are wired for that. Journaling is a way of assuming control, first by identifying and labeling what I am thinking that's causing me to feel fear, then by assuming responsibility for how I plan to address that fear.

Once I can clearly identify what I am thinking and get some distance from my perception, I can see it out on paper and consider, from a more objective point of view, if I agree with those thoughts or ideas, if I think that they serve me, or if it's time to seek out an alternative and try on a different way of thinking about whatever I see as the source or cause of my fear.

In our current political climate, there is constant fear. How do you create despite that?

Aris Mejias: The uncertainty of our political climate in the US has been something quite consistent for way more years in Puerto Rico. We have had a colonial situation in our country since 1899. There has been consistent divisions in politics, social fabric, and ideologies. Our economy is fragmented, and we have no control over it. Yet in the midst of all this, we create aggressively. Puerto Rico is rich in culture and arts. It is the only thing no external structure can control. So we use it. We exploit it to the last of its fibers. It is our survival.

Sara Eve Rivera: Creation is my escape in this overwhelming social-political state of turmoil, judgment, and hate. While tattooing, my client and I are focusing so intensely on the moment at hand. Though we may talk about politics or current events, we are very much isolated from the outer world. I wanted to create a space where

people can discuss their opinions without explosive judgment. I want the shop to still feel relevant and connected to the outside world, but at the same time to feel more like a pause button from the stressors, even if only for a moment.

Rooney Elmi: Since I tend to channel fear into creative channels, it's actually a direct source of inspiration rather than a determinant. On the one-year anniversary of Trump's inauguration, *SVLLY(wood)*, my movie magazine, dedicated its sophomore issue to examining a cinematic uprising's past, present, and future. Like I said in the editor's note, "In times of political crisis, it's vital to remember that art is the soul of the revolution."

Shannon Mustipher: The state of our world, the politics—it motivates me to do something positive. We not only need to call out and work to correct those things that are harming society, but to be intentional about bringing positive energy and change to the world. I regard my work as a way of serving others. If I do well in my work, someone may learn from me and do even better than I did. If I help a client improve their product or service, then their end customer gets more value and a better experience. It goes on and on. With so much destruction and threats to our collective safety in the world, creating is imperative, a responsibility to do one's part—now more than ever.

As confidence grows, does fear recede or simply change?

Annie Selke: Confidence comes from conquering fear. So if you do conquer the same fear repeatedly, it gets a little easier every time (except, for me, the public-speaking fear). I suppose you are getting progressively more comfortable with the fear because you have a better understanding of the outcome.

Rae Tutera: For me, fear just changes shape. I have what I consider to be more "mature" fears than I used to have.

Aris Mejias: Wow. Age does play a factor in my choices. I am bolder, less blindly agreeable, persistent, and loud. I am happy with making wrong decisions and easily moving forward. It usually boils down to making the decisions that tire me the least. This has been applied to friendships, work situations, even designs.

Sara Eve Rivera: Being heavily tattooed, especially as a non-binary or female-identifying person, is often closely associated with "body politics." By doing so, we are publicly and very verbally labeled as a "millennial," a "liberal," an "outsider," etc. I feel that my very appearance and way of life serves as its own version of protest and resistance; reclaiming my own body with permanent marks as I see fit. I have received very mixed reactions to my appearance. But I was able to move beyond fear

of judgment by becoming tattooed. Instead of seeing a publicly judged physical body, I saw a body covered in art that I love and appreciate. It made me feel more comfortable with myself, more confident in myself.

Shannon Mustipher: It changes. Having more confidence is the result of having tried and succeeded at something new, which leads me to attempt the next new thing—something out of my comfort zone, something outside of my experience, something that is beyond my current skill set. When venturing into uncharted territory, it's natural that fear would enter the picture. I've learned to accept—and even embrace—it as a sign that I am being faced with an opportunity to grow and become a better person.

How do you move beyond fear, and how would you encourage others to do so?

Annie Selke: Do your best work! That is all you can ask of yourself.

Rae Tutera: I couldn't move beyond fear, or anything else that weighs me down, without others. I encourage people to cultivate the relationships that help them feel rooted and safe, so that they can experience truth and be brave. I would be remiss if I didn't mention the fact that I have a therapist and a partner who help me dismantle my fears so I can not only be present in my own life, but be present in others' lives, too.

Aris Mejias: I am no therapist, but I would blindly recommend taking a walk in the park, lying in the grass, and looking at the stars. If you are able to see the bigger picture and position yourself within that, you have gained a step ahead of fear.

Sara Eve Rivera: I would recommend that to move beyond fear in these uncertain times, each person can look at their own skill set and community and find small or large ways to be the change. Find ways to change your communities for the better and take things in bite-size pieces. Creating positive change is incredibly empowering.

Rooney Elmi: Remembering that this too is temporary.

Shannon Mustipher: JUST DO IT. Keep it simple. Understand that fear comes with the territory of doing what needs to be done to be a better person. Be honest about where you are with the people who can encourage you and support you—and get ready to surprise yourself and discover that you are more of a badass than you think! **gc**

Annie Segarra

YouTube star, artist, and activist Annie Segarra discusses the future of accessibility and the importance of fostering community.

By Kayla Whaley
Photo collage by Dana Fortune

Annie Segarra (better known on YouTube as Annie Elainey) has a magnetic presence. Her penchant for brightly colored hair certainly helps, but it's her delivery and command of the camera that truly captivate the viewer. Whether she's dissecting casually ableist language, sharing her journey to diagnosis, or vlogging about a day out with her sister, Segarra's videos are intimate, compelling, and an utter joy to watch.

A queer, Latinx, disabled, and chronically ill woman, Segarra is known for her incisive social justice commentary and her talent for sparking viral—and vital—conversations like #TheFutureIsAccessible and #HotPersonInAWheelchair. These hashtags, like Segarra's videos, are powerful not only because of their content, but also because they invite others to join in, creating a loud, sometimes dissonant, always beautiful chorus of disabled voices. No matter the medium, Segarra's work seems to be as much about fostering community as it is about spreading awareness.

In a video about Frida Kahlo that highlights the iconic artist's disabilities, Segarra says she found "validation, solidarity, and inspiration from [Kahlo's] life story and

from her art." When I watched that video, the idea of inspiration being tied explicitly to a sense of kinship hit me hard. "Inspiration" has long been weaponized against disabled people (the late activist Stella Young's TED Talk on "inspiration porn" is an excellent introduction to that history), so to hear Segarra reclaim that word and reframe it in a context of community struck me as wildly powerful. It also struck me as exceptionally fitting, because through her activism and online presence, Segarra is following in Kahlo's metaphorical footsteps by inspiring me and countless other disabled women to be proud, bold, and real.

I want to start by talking about activism generally. How do you define activism? What does it look like in your life?

Activism, to me, revolves around the idea of justice. When I was a teenager, I definitely saw activism as equivalent to being a protester. I figured, if you're an activist, you're out there and you're protesting in the street for what you believe in, right? But my idea of activism changed [after I became physically disabled] when I realized the impact I still had even though I wasn't physically

out in the streets anymore. So my form of activism has been my visibility. To the untrained mind, that doesn't really make any sense. "You exist, so you're an activist?" But it's more about being loud about your existence, specifically when you're multiply marginalized.

For a long time, my activism was very White Feminism–focused. Even though I identify as queer, I didn't realize how my intersecting identities were dismissed or ignored within that brand of feminism. And I wasn't really conscious of disability issues until I became disabled myself.

That's extremely disappointing for me, because my younger sister/best friend is autistic, and I've advocated for her in a bunch of spaces, but my knowledge about disability was very basic and focused simply on antibullying. It wasn't until I became disabled myself that I realized that even though I love my disabled sister, I still held ableist belief systems! I realized I sometimes infantilized my sister because of her disability. I had to ask myself, *Am I babying you because you're my baby sister, or because you're disabled?*

When I started using a wheelchair, suddenly the entire way I moved through the world, interacted with the world, interacted with people—that all changed. Because I was using the wheelchair, people would ignore me and would ask my sister where I would like to sit or if I was okay, etc.

So that's all been tough, and it took me sitting in a wheelchair and seeing how people treated me so differently to realize there's this whole new ball game I wasn't aware of. I needed to listen to other disabled people and their experiences, and to really be in the moment of my own experiences.

You say your activism is largely about visibility, but it also sounds very heavily rooted in this deep introspection. I think there's a really interesting tension there between being externally focused but internally driven.

I'm a very introspective person, and I know I take all my experience and examine myself hard, but I hadn't thought of it like that before! I think that introspection probably is the core action of my activism. If there's one thing I'd want my activism to accomplish, it would be for everyone to just sit with themselves for a moment. Some people are born disabled, and others, like me, have disability thrust upon them. So I know what those abled privileges are from experience, and losing those privileges is difficult. I'm honestly glad it happened to me, though, because I was already an activist, I was already voicing my thoughts and opinions, my experiences, in an effort to build empathy and justice. And disability has now become my main focus, especially because I feel like it's been on the back burner for too long—not just in my own activism, but in activism, period. Activism

communities say they believe in equality and inclusion, but accessibility isn't considered very often, so disabled people are excluded from those spaces. Which doesn't really fit well with the stated values of those communities.

We live in a system and a society that constantly holds disabled people as an afterthought. Hopefully my videos and vocal online presence can help move disabled people to the forefront where we belong.

You have an undeniable charisma on screen that's such a joy to watch, but I'm curious: What drew you to videos in the first place? Was it that desire to be visible? Something else?

I've been involved in theater, acting, performing, basically my entire life. I think I was like three or four years old and already singing musical pieces into a video camera. So that's just innate in me. I've been documenting things on film for a big part of my life and I think it's the way I communicate best. Videos just feel more intimate to me [than other media].

I also like being able to speak to two audiences at the same time. Videos let me easily flip back and forth between speaking to my community and speaking to people outside my community, and viewers understand immediately who I'm addressing at any given moment. Those transitions feel more difficult to pull off with writing, where you don't have the benefit of tonality, facial expressions, the sound of my voice.

I want to talk about "The Future Is Accessible." You coined the phrase

as a response to the inaccessibility you saw at the Women's March, and it's become this hugely resonant online campaign. Why do you think it's struck such a chord with so many, so fast? Has the response matched your original vision for it?**

I didn't really have a vision for it! I created it as sort of a protest sign, my way of participating in a march that wasn't accessible to me. I'm genuinely surprised it's resonated with so many people the way that it has. I think maybe part of why it's taken off is because accessibility is something most people can get behind, once it's brought to their attention, whether they're disabled or not. I think it speaks to something most people want: a future that is more inclusive, that everyone can participate in, that everyone can thrive in. I think it's exciting to consider an accessible future—it's optimistic, it's joyful, it's empowering. I know that's how I feel when I wear the shirt: I feel empowered to advocate for myself, empowered to demand accessibility.

It's also a play off the seventies feminist slogan "The Future Is Female." I think there's something beautiful and powerful about the temporal interplay of that reframing. Can you talk a little about that? I'm also curious about how you think feminism in particular can grapple with its historical ableism while working toward an accessible future. How do you see that playing out?

I think feminism, like society as a whole, has a lot of learning and improving to do in regards to accessibility. Feminism often leaves disability on the back burner, out of sight, out of mind, and by reframing "The Future Is Female" to "The Future Is Accessible," I demand to take up space and to be visible as a disabled woman in feminist spaces. I did something similar with my "Nobody Knows I Have EDS" campaign for EDS Awareness Month, inspired by "Nobody Knows I'm Gay," because I feel like the invisibility of my queerness is very much comparable to the invisibility of my illness. These intersections are *way* more common than the non-disabled members of these communities like to believe.

Do you find there's an added level of emotional consequence when your exclusion comes at the hands of another of your marginalized communities?

Definitely! There is pain in the hypocrisy. Like I said earlier, feminist spaces and LGBTQIA+ spaces have this song and dance of "We're all family, all equal, all welcome," but we're not treated that way. I've had experiences with inaccessible feminist events and gay bars alike. I've confronted inaccessibility in certain spaces to no avail, and that strikes a real mighty blow—it reads as a dismissal of our right to be in these spaces. It literally impacts our ability to be among our community. We are not equal, we are not welcome, and we definitely don't feel like family.

I want to shift gears a bit. "Bravery" is often a fraught descriptor in the disabled community because of the

ableist ways it's been used against us historically. What does living a brave life mean to you outside an ableist context?**

For me, vulnerability is bravery. I think sometimes in response to ableist prejudices, many of us have this tendency to overcompensate, which manifests as a hyper-focus on "ability." We sometimes feel this need to prove our worth and our joy to non-disabled people. I think it's brave to allow ourselves to be real. We're allowed to love ourselves, our lives, and our bodies, and still be honest about the hard parts, about the injustices, about our frustrations with our bodies. Our experiences are multidimensional, and I think it's very brave to treat them as such.

How do you handle the unique pressures, stresses, and fears of being an online personality?

I think my biggest online anxieties are about being wrong or making a mistake, but I'm quickly learning that when we do mess up, what matters is how we handle it. We apologize, correct it, and move forward. I also make sure I step back from creating when I'm going through a depressive episode. My logical side understands that sharing the toxic things my depression comes up with wouldn't be wise, especially with my influential platforms.

Speaking of depression, I'd actually like to focus on some of the fears and anxieties that come with being disabled rather than those that come with being online. Most people would probably say the loss of ability

is a scary thing to think about. As a person with a degenerative disease, I've had to learn to accept that as a part of my life, which isn't to say I'm not scared of future changes—I am. But there's a small part of me that also feels ready, because I've built a solid foundation and sense of self rooted in the body peace I found after body dysmorphic disorder/eating disorder recovery, and equally rooted in the representation I found in communities like #CripplePunk. Ultimately that's why I feel visibility for my community and for myself as a disabled person is so vital. Losing abilities is scary. It's scary to lose things, to have to mourn things, to lose privileges and opportunities, to lose friends, to have to relearn how to live your life, to relearn how to move through the world. There is a huge social fear of becoming disabled, and I felt it, too, especially when I first started using a wheelchair. But I ultimately landed safely in the arms of my community.

Online I found examples of personhood with disability, examples of strength, ferocity, creativity, and accessibility. Witnessing positive and authentic representations of disability was so affirming and empowering for me. I hope that through my own visibility and authenticity, I'm able to be that for others: an example of disability without shame. I want people to know the resources available to them as disabled people, to know there is a community for them. I want them to know disabled lives are worth living, that they deserve their rights, and that they are worthy of taking up space in this world. **gc**

The Butterfly Effect

Meet the Radical Monarchs, the next generation of young women working to change their communities and the world at large.

By Meg José Mateo
Photography by Gabriela Hasbun

Radical Healing. Radical Self-Love. Black Lives Matter. Radical Pride. **These are just a few of the badges that adorn the vests of the Radical Monarchs. Made up of young women of color ages eight to fourteen, this girls' group moves beyond simple volunteerism, sewing crafts, and outdoor education—components typical of traditional girls' groups—to learn** about what it's like to really stand up for your community.

The idea for the group came about in early 2014 when Anayvette Martinez's daughter Lupita was in fourth grade. At the time, Lupita wanted to join her local Girl Scouts troop. But Anayvette didn't think it would speak to her daughter's experience, especially after hearing that the group was not diverse. A community worker for local youth, Anayvette wanted something more for her daughter; something that connected to the socially conscious values of their family and centered on the experiences of young girls of color. Anayvette daydreamed about what a troop like that might look like, and even what types of badges they might get. It sent her mind whirling. "I mentioned

Lupita Martinez,
Juliana Contreras &
Sabina Contreras

Namixtulu
Esteva

the idea to my daughter, and she was really into it," Anayvette says. "My life was busy and months went by, but Lupita never forgot. I told my friend Marilyn Hollinquest about it—and she thought it was an amazing idea." Marilyn, a middle school teacher and community advocate, and Anayvette got to work. In December of that year, Radical Brownies (the group's initial name) was born. The first troop began with Lupita and her friends, but grew to include more girls from the Oakland community.

The news of the group made instant headlines—"Badges for Badasses"—and spurred Fox News host Sean Hannity to surmise, "We think the girls are being exploited." While Radical Monarchs provides an alternative to the Girl Scouts, it's not as if they were the first to create such an option. Multiple girls' groups with badge-filled vests exist—from Camp Fire and Frontier Girls to American Heritage Girls, which has a conservative Christian focus—but no one has attempted what Radical Monarchs are going for: a girls' group with a social justice foundation focusing on issues that affect young women of color.

"There's a lot of rampant injustice happening. We have to teach young people how to be advocates and allies in order to be in community with each other and achieve social justice," states Marilyn. For the group, Anayvette and Marilyn generate curriculum related to timely issues in the national conversation and what's going on in the girls' lives, as well as anything the girls want to work on. They set each unit to last about three months, with the culmination of their learning manifesting in an activity or a project like screen-printing posters (for their "Radical Roots" unit) or making flower essence sprays and herbal first-aid kits (for their "Radical Healing" unit).

In many ways, the cofounders are creating an experience and a sisterhood that they wish they had had themselves at that age. "I made these types of connections, but much later in life," says Anayvette. "What would it look like for an eight-, nine-, or ten-year-old to make those types connections now rather than waiting until college?"

Born in San Francisco, Anayvette, thirty-four, is of Central American descent. Her father emigrated from El Salvador in the early 1970s, and her mother is a first-generation Nicaraguan American, the first in her family to be born in the States. "My mother was born in San Francisco and was actually in the Girl Scouts in the 1950s. She was the only person of color in the group," Anayvette recalls. "I can only imagine how it was for her back then."

Anayvette and her family moved around the city's neighborhoods—Sunset, Excelsior, Mission—all throughout the eighties and early nineties, their living situation constantly threatened by spreading gentrification. When Anayvette was in the seventh grade, the dot-com bubble burst; her parents lost their jobs and decided to move to Miami. She returned to California for college, graduating from UCLA, where she majored in Chicano studies and minored in women's studies. At San Francisco State University (SFSU), she completed a master's in ethnic studies in 2007.

While at SFSU, she met Marilyn, who was in the same program. "Marilyn and I instantly connected. We shared identities as queer women of color, passionate values rooted in social justice, and even a birthday!" Anayvette remembers.

Radical Monarchs cofounder Marilyn Hollinquest, thirty-eight, hails from California's Central Valley. She grew up in Tulare, but was born in Hanford, a rural farming town where generations of her parents' families had lived since the Great Migration. The oldest of five siblings, Marilyn was raised in a single-parent household after she lost her father. When she was in fourth grade, her family moved to Sacramento because her mother wanted more job opportunities beyond the limited agricultural and retail offerings in Tulare.

In Sacramento, her mom was able to get certificates to serve in various medical capacities, including working in a nursing home and doing medical billing and coding. She often worked multiple jobs. Watching her mother, Marilyn struggled to understand the inequalities they experienced. "I saw how hard my mother worked, how much overtime she put in," she says. "I would see other people's parents, and they seemed to be able to be around more and work less and have more money. People would say, 'Work hard,' but my mom *was* working hard and her ends weren't meeting. I wondered why that was happening." It was these types of experiences and questions growing up that led Marilyn to pursue a degree in community studies at UC Santa Cruz and a master's in ethnic studies from SFSU.

During its first three years, Radical Monarchs remained a side project and difficult to juggle for both Anayvette and Marilyn. In July 2017, Anayvette was laid off from her day job. "The layoff was very

Styling by Keri Henderson; makeup by Andrea C. Samuels

Scaru Esteva
& Amia
Ramanathan

Marilyn
Hollinquest
(Cofounder)

Xander
Asamamlay
(Marilyn's
husband)

Amia Ramanathan,
Namixtulu Esteva,
Lupita Martinez &
Neveah Kelly

unexpected," she says. "But I took it as a sign from the universe, because I wanted to do Radical Monarchs full-time." Things began wondrously falling into place soon thereafter: In November, the Radical Monarchs received a grant that budgeted for the duo to work on Radical Monarchs full-time. With that, they took on specific titles: Anayvette as CEO of programs and communications and Marilyn as CEO of finance and operations.

In June 2018, inaugural Troop #1 graduated, ending their year with a "Radical Media" unit in which each girl had the choice to make a short film, zine, or podcast for their final project. The big event included keynotes by Alicia Garza, a cofounder of Black Lives Matter, and Isa Noyola, a national translatina activist. Looking back over the past three years, Anayvette and Marilyn recognize the girls' transformation. "We saw them develop and flourish, rooted in who they are and in their voices and being advocates for themselves and their community," Anayvette says. "But we didn't make them fierce. They came in as fierce girls already." **gc**

Stay Awake

Artist Lisa Congdon's graphic art has been a rallying cry for the state of our political union. Here we collected a few of our favorite pieces for you to be inspired and galvanized by.

Unapologetically HER

Author, activist, and founder of Equality for HER, Blair Imani talks about life at the intersection of Black, queer, and Muslim identity—and how she's found strength to persevere through harrowing situations.

By Grace Bonney
Photography by Myles Loftin

What is your relationship to fear, and how have you found the courage to stand up in situations that can be dangerous, both literally and figuratively?

Fear is something that I grapple with daily. Whether it's the fear of impostor syndrome, where I worry that I will disappoint myself, others, or my family, or the concern that my public visibility will bring about physical harm to myself or my loved ones—fear is something that is an intimate part of my life. From the chemical standpoint, I have been prescribed anxiety medication to help my brain discern the actual fears from the less practical ones.

What does your support system look like? Who are the people and what are the tools you lean on when you face difficult moments in life and work?

I have such a vast and multifaceted support system. It's made up of people I've known my entire life, like my mom, dad, and siblings, but it's also made up of people who I have never met in real life—people who I know from the internet and from sites like Instagram and Twitter. I think that having the ability to make friends who live across the country or in the same city who you've never met really redefines what a support system is. My support system is made up of familiar faces and complete strangers—all of whom are concerned about my well-being and long-term happiness.

What is something you know now about life and/or your work that you wish you'd known five or ten years ago?

Ten years ago, when I was a teenager, it would've been nice to know that I would be okay. I placed so much of my value in external validation and I'm glad that I no longer believe that's where my worth comes from. At fourteen or fifteen, the entire world felt like it was falling apart for me. Had I known that it wasn't the end of the world to struggle making friends, getting good grades, or impressing the cool kids, I think I would've been a much happier and more extroverted kiddo.

What did you want to be when you were a child? Did you ever see yourself doing what you do now?

When I was a kid I very much wanted to be a lawyer. That might've been because I saw *Legally Blonde* a few too many times or because I grew up going to church with civil rights lawyers like Johnny Cochran. I wanted to change the world for the better, and I feel I am doing that today. The difference is that I now understand one doesn't have to work "within" the system as a lawyer or lawmaker to create change.

What is the hardest thing about the work you do that people may not expect?

As a public figure and activist, the hardest thing is that I am so accessible to so many

I hope people see me and understand that you can unapologetically be yourself.

people. On certain days that's a beautiful thing, but often it means that people who have abused me in the past are able to keep up with me with a simple Google search and that is scary. It is something I try not to think about, but it's a reality.

What characteristic of yourself are you proudest of?

I am proud that I get to be myself in public almost all the time. I never imagined that the weird things about me—like how I can conjure up conspiracy theories about any breaking news story or how I can dampen a mood in an instant with facts and figures about human rights atrocities—would be interesting or desirable to other people. I never thought that being myself would give strength to others to do the same. I'm proud of that!

The differences between our online and offline lives can sometimes be significant. And sharing truly vulnerable moments can change the way we are perceived. How do you manage that offline/online perception and the pressure that can come with being viewed as a role model to so many?

I may regret it in the future, but I try to be myself both online and offline 100 percent. Feminista Jones taught me that it's important to create a personal brand that is a reflection of your true self or else you'll run the risk of resenting who you are. If trolls or haters are ruining my mood, I'll post about it. If I'm enjoying a family moment, I'll post about it (within reason). I try not to do things like put on a hijab

for the sake of posting a photo if I wasn't already wearing one that day. Sometimes that authenticity pisses people off but I'm not doing it for them, I'm doing it for me. If I happen to inspire people along the way then *Alhamdulillah*, that's beautiful.

How do you feel about labels in relation to your life and work? Some people proudly claim them, while others feel they hinder their work and message. What are your feelings about identity labels in today's world?

In today's world having identity labels makes it very easy for people to classify and categorize you. On the other hand, it makes it easy for people to find you. Before I went to Kenya, I had my identifiers listed in my Twitter and Instagram bios, but now I've listed that I am a flower with many petals, which I believe is a more poetic way of telling people that I'm beautifully complex.

Can you walk us through a moment when something did not go as planned and what you learned from that?

I think that when I was arrested in Baton Rouge, Louisiana, in July 2016, that was an example of something not going according to plan *whatsoever*. I've taught classes [at colleges] on civil disobedience and the proper way to "take an arrest." However, when I got arrested in Baton Rouge, I was totally unprepared, and it was as if I had never taken any courses on simple disobedience. Small things—like wearing a wireless bra or setting up a bail fund and wearing white—all went out the door because the situation escalated so quickly. It

taught me that the unexpected will happen, especially when you are at the whims of those in power.

Do you have fears or professional challenges that keep you up at night? How do you put them to bed and find time to restore and renew yourself?

I keep a Notes app or screenshot journal of receipts of my success. Impostor syndrome exists because people outside of the status quo are told their whole lives that [they] cannot be successful. But I *am* successful and I remind myself by keeping track of those successes, so if doubt creeps into my mind I can just open my phone and remind myself that I'm kick-ass.

Where do you feel most alive, and why?

I feel most alive when I'm back home in California swimming in the pool with my younger cousins. When I hang out with my family, I'm not dealing with the stress of being a public figure. I'm just Blair and I like that.

What message or feeling do you hope people take away from your work, your words, and your example?

I hope people see me and understand that you can unapologetically be yourself.

Blair Imani's first book, Modern HERstory: Stories of Women and Nonbinary People Rewriting History *(Ten Speed Press), will be out on October 16, 2018.* 🦶

STAMP OF APPROVAL

by Sarah Neuburger

I made stamps and sold them.

They were popular in big, tiny ways.

An email came that a national retail store was considering placing an order.

My stamps could be in stores everywhere. I saw it. I loved it.

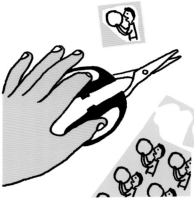

But I was cutting the rubber by hand, which meant I couldn't discount the cost so the store did not buy them.

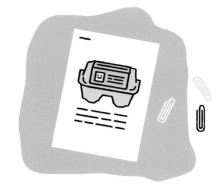

I saw my limitations. I wrote a proposal to have someone else manufacture the stamps for me.

Chronicle Books, at the time, was making stamp sets so I sent my proposal to them.

They liked it. And then I waited and waited and waited. I signed with a book agent to keep following up with them.

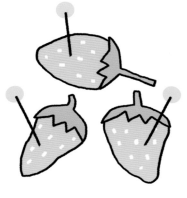

We couldn't pin down what we would create together. The stamp set wasn't what they wanted to publish.

Eventually, Chronicle Books called and we decided on our first formats to be published.

I was thrilled. My agent said we have an offer and contract coming soon.

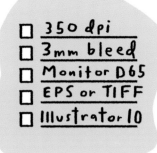

☐ 350 dpi
☐ 3mm bleed
☐ Monitor D65
☐ EPS or TIFF
☐ Illustrator 10

After negotiating a few points, the contract and list of deliverables arrived. I read it.

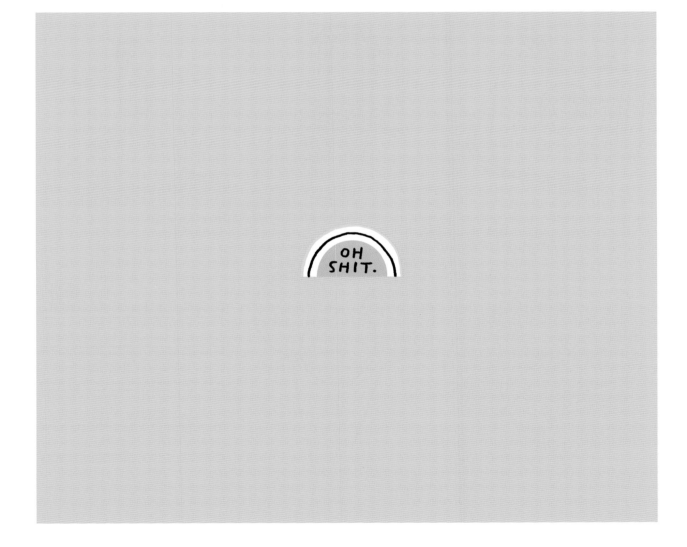

OH SHIT.

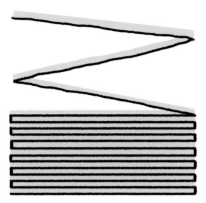

The contract was so long and detailed CMYK limitations and computer monitor calibrations.

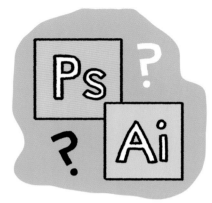

The delivery requirements listed computer programs I did not own or know how to use.

My computer may have well been from 1976. It had a space bar but not much else.

My digital camera was still new, which meant I no longer had to develop photos at CVS and scan them to post on my blog.

Can I agree to do this? The choice was mine: Shit or get off the pot.

Done. Let's go. I can do this.

I signed the contract.

Celebration occurred. I was proud.

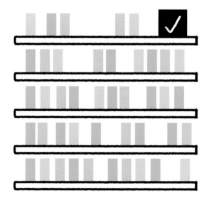

Afterward, I promptly stuck the art delivery checklist on the top shelf of my mind for a while.

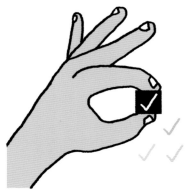

The time came to take the unknown scary off the top shelf and figure this mess out.

I knocked on doors and did a lot of internet searching. I also got my own copy of Photoshop.

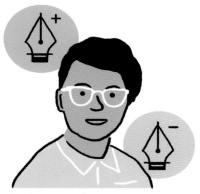

I had a dear friend who owned Illustrator so we sat down and stumbled through the rest.

Eventually, my drawings were in digital files named things they wanted with specs they requested and I was relieved.

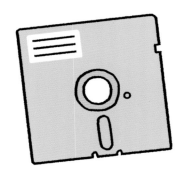

I sent them off afraid they might see it was saved on a floppy disk from my 1976 computer. (Not exactly true but felt like it.)

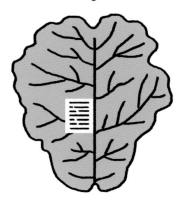

Or it could have been microfilm that I implanted in a fiddle leaf given the lack of proficiency I felt with what I delivered.

Nothing awful happened except something amazing. My gift and stationery collection was published!

It took a while to no longer feel like a fraud and create a system for how I work digitally but I got there.

I realized I wasn't a fraud. I was what I needed to be: optimistic, scrappy, and resourceful. Go for it! You got this. _Sn_

Paula Scher

An interview with the legendary designer who believes the best work happens outside of your comfort zone.

By Debbie Millman
Photography by Ike Edeani

The design work of Paula Scher has made an undeniable imprint on the visual culture of our time. Her early record covers for Atlantic and CBS Records remain classics of the genre, their intelligence and wit poignant to this day. Her work for arts organizations such as the Public Theater, the Metropolitan Opera, and the Museum of Modern Art showcase an ability to capture the vitality of her subject matter with heady assemblages of type and image. Her work for global organizations such as Citi and Microsoft reveal her deft hand at corporate branding.

Paula is perhaps best known for her use of type, but she's told me that it wasn't until after college that she came to understand typography. "I didn't seek it," she explains. "It found me." Paula's success seems inevitable and effortless, but nothing could be further from the truth. She began her design career when women were unlikely leaders in the discipline, yet she has maintained a level of accomplishment in the field that is unprecedented. Paula seems to be able to do it all: she is a designer, a fine artist, a typographer, a writer, and a partner in the world's largest independent design firm, Pentagram. There she has broken new ground in graphic design, exhibition design, installation design, and more.

She is also an educator; her teaching career includes over two decades at the School of Visual Arts, along with positions at the Cooper Union and Yale. Last year, Unit Editions published *Paula Scher: Works*, a 520-page chronological visual record spanning Paula's career to date. In our interview at Pentagram's New York office, we sat in the late morning sunlight and talked about fear, risk, criticism, and reinvention.

Fear is a really complicated topic. There are external things that can scare us—like accidents and rabid animals—and there are internal things that scare us—like vulnerability and

shame. Can you talk to me about how fear has impacted your life?

In many ways, fear has been a motivating factor: I didn't have a great childhood. I was battling my parents—my parents were big, and I was little. It took courage to stand up to them, and somewhere along the way I made the choice that it was better to battle them than to let them mold me in the way they wanted to mold me. Initially I did this without a lot of confidence; I just forced myself to do it. It motivated me to go to art school, to move to New York, to put myself in situations that were scary, and to handle all kinds of sexism.

How were your parents trying to mold you?

I grew up in the fifties and sixties. I lived in the suburbs, where everybody behaved the same way. They all looked the same, they dressed the same, and they went to the same schools. They went to the same church or synagogue. They all belonged to the same kinds of clubs. There were expected ways of dressing. I didn't conform to any of it and I felt like a failure. I felt like I didn't look appropriate and I didn't fit in. But when I was sixteen, I got a job working in a shoe store—then I could buy clothes. That was my beginning of my working life, and I've been working ever since.

When people are afraid of things or are being forced to do things, there's any

number of responses they can have. What gave you your defiance?

I tried it their way, and it didn't work for me. I knew I was different from the people I went to high school with. I felt like I was smarter than a lot of the people I met, and I cared about things they didn't care about.

I did have a few teachers who were very supportive of me. They saved my life. I had an English teacher who realized I could write. She took one of my short stories and entered it into the *Atlantic Monthly* competition and it won an honorable mention. I didn't even know I had that kind of capability! It was the first prize I ever won. And it gave me a sense of possibility.

You were—and still are—a pioneer. You entered the design business at a time when there were very few women in leadership positions. You entered the field and not only broke new ground but were recognized very early on. What gave you the confidence to talk about your work, to command the respect that you did, and—in many ways—fly in the face of so much sexism at that time?

I was lucky in the timing. Historically, what I think men have been better at is not the accomplishment, but rather the retaining of credit for their work. Some of the ability to sustain a long career is managing the difficulty of the practice itself. In order to sustain a long-term career, you have to

be willing to make changes all along the way. You have to be willing to analyze what you're doing and how to grow it in relationship to your time. That's the only way you can continually maintain a visible output over, say, four decades. If you stay exactly where you are, and you do the same thing over and over, you are going to fade away.

You have been working at the top of your field for five decades.

But who's counting? [*laughter*]

You've done that, in large part, by what seems to be effortlessly reinventing your body of work. You became well-known as a designer in the music business. Then you became a solo practitioner. You joined Pentagram in 1991. Then you vastly expanded the type of work you were doing at Pentagram. Then you became a successful painter. You have essentially conquered every discipline of design! But I've noticed that once you've reached a certain level of mastery—rather than rinse, repeat, rinse, repeat—you've gone on to conquer another facet of design wherein you had no track record and no reputation. And you've been successful and hit it out of the ballpark again and again! And you have yet to peak!
   Where do you get the courage to say, "You know what? I'm done with

If you stay exactly where you are, and you do the same thing over and over, you are going to fade away.

records. I want to do *this* now. I'm done with books. I want to do *that* now. I'm done with museums. Now I want to do *this*!" Where does that courage come from?

I worked in the record industry when I was very young. It was during a time where, financially, one year was better than the next. Then in the late seventies/early eighties, the record industry crashed. Shortly thereafter, I left. First and foremost, I left because it became an unpleasant place to work. Also, I knew that CDs were going to replace album covers and I didn't have any interest in

designing them. But I learned lessons from these things: When the financial climate becomes bad, the politics become bad. People are fearful. You can't design or make any kind of headway in a period of fear. If you're in a corporation and the people are all fearful about being fired, they're only going to be able to do whatever they think they need to do to save their positions. It means they'll never take any risks.

It also means that if somebody in a higher position says, "This is the way it should be," nobody is going to challenge it. It's a really bad place to work and a very bad place for creativity. At that point in my career, I'd

made miles of record covers. I didn't want to make squares anymore. I wanted to be able to do other things. But I can't say that I was fearless when I left; I was really afraid.

But I remember talking to Colin Forbes at the time and he told me something that made so much sense, even though I didn't feel it at the time. He said that if I had a job, I essentially had one client. If I lost that client, I would be helpless. But if I was on my own, I might have two, three, or four clients. The likelihood of losing them all at the same time was not realistic. So even though I didn't believe it emotionally, he persuaded me that I was more secure being on my own—freelancing—than I would ever be working for an employer.

Did you have a sense that you could rely on yourself?

I didn't think that I had any choice. But I did a couple of very smart things. I reasoned that I could get book-jacket work, because it was similar to record-cover work. Sure enough, I could. I went around with my record-cover portfolio. I got work almost immediately. But it was hard not to know exactly how much money I was going to earn in a year. I had to take a leap of faith.

Yet you are restless. Do you get bored with mastery and then feel like you need to conquer something new? What gives you your sensitivity to keep trying new things?

I think work informs work. I'm interested in personal growth. I'm interested in what I can discover as a designer. I know that I can't follow fads, because if I follow fads, I'm a follower and not a leader. I also know that the work has to evolve. It has to inform and evolve. Generally, you learn things from going outside your comfort zone. You learn things by being a neophyte. But it *is* scary.

Do you feel nervous when starting something new that you don't know how to do?

Yes. But I don't let nervousness stop me. Because of my experience, I reason that I can do something if I've done it before. If I haven't done it before, and I really want to do it, I will muster all of my forces and say, "I can do this because I want to do this." When I put myself in that position, I will succeed at it. But I don't always do that. Sometimes, it just doesn't seem worth it. It takes the energy of a twenty-year-old to have that kind of arrogance.

How do you mitigate criticism as you break new ground? People respond to change with tremendous fear. Yet you do it over and over again and are continually being criticized for doing something new that nobody has seen before. Then it's just a matter of time before everybody is doing it. How do you cope?

It's really, really crazy. People will threaten murder over changing the tail of a tiger in the logo of a sports team. You have to realize when you have rabid fans—in any industry—you're going to be upsetting them by changing something they are used to seeing. But you must remember that it will dissipate, because those people do, in fact, go away. When you're designing for a school, as I did for [the] Parsons/The New School [logo] (which got tremendous backlash), you're not designing for this year's students. You're designing for the next group of students.

But the real takeaway is this: I have to get anything new approved. In the case of the Parsons/The New School logo, I had forty people on a committee signing off on it: deans in every school, the heads of the school, *and* outside donors. The whole community had to be involved, the entire school community. It was a long, arduous process of getting the identity approved.

When the backlash occurred, they supported the work because they had all been part of it. They believed in what we created together. I realized at that moment that this stuff matters. And then, a year later, it all went away. We live in a time where it is easy to put something down. To be able to explain why something is working and something is good takes analysis and time. To trash something, well, you just need an iPhone and the internet. If it's easy to tweet some piece of nastiness about something in two seconds [while you're] on the toilet, why wouldn't you?

In the meantime, in New York City alone I think I've seen at least ten variations on the typography and logo you did for Parsons/The New School.

Good. If people copy what I do, they have the opportunity to do it better. The "first one" of anything is usually lousy because it takes a certain period of time to actually develop the craft of it. [*laughs*]

Yet you're not afraid to put the work out there.

No. I'm much more interested in the moment of making a discovery. Also, that type of craft—to really perfect something—takes patience that I don't have. I really don't have a lot of patience; after I have an idea and it's out there, that's when I get bored and want to do something new. **gc**

Jamie Okuma

Fashion designer Jamie Okuma discusses how she finds strength and courage in family heritage and her indigenous community.

By Chelsey Luger
Photography by Matika Wilbur
Beadwork photography by Cameron Linton

If you're at all familiar with North American indigenous beadwork, particularly if you've ever tried to learn it or if you comprehend the process behind its creation, you probably have an immense appreciation for it. Each tiny bead represents an intentional decision by the artist and at least a moment of the artist's time. Often, one single piece will be composed of thousands of these beads, these decisions, these moments.

Jamie Okuma is, quite honestly, a beadwork goddess. Her work is well-known and widely recognized in First Nations and Native American circles, and she is also sought after in fine art markets and the museum world (for example, a little place called the Met). If you've ever seen a Christian Louboutin shoe marvelously adorned in indigenous design, that's Okuma.

But beadwork is by no means all she does. On any given day, you might find her super-momming—homeschooling her boys on the La Jolla Indian Reservation in Southern California, where she was born and raised and remains a committed and active member of the community. From there, she also runs her e-commerce business, where she sells originally designed clothing and accessories, like her immensely popular brightly colored floral leggings. She also works continually on her other fine art endeavors, of which there are many.

I've known of Jamie's work for a long time, so I was thrilled to be able to sit down with her for this interview and get to know the woman behind the beads.

Describe, in your own words, what you do.

I do what I love! What I've loved since I was five years old, actually, and now I get to do it for a living. I'm a multidisciplinary artist. I don't like to nail down the "type" of art that I do, but I would say that I'm best known for my beadwork. Although, professionally,

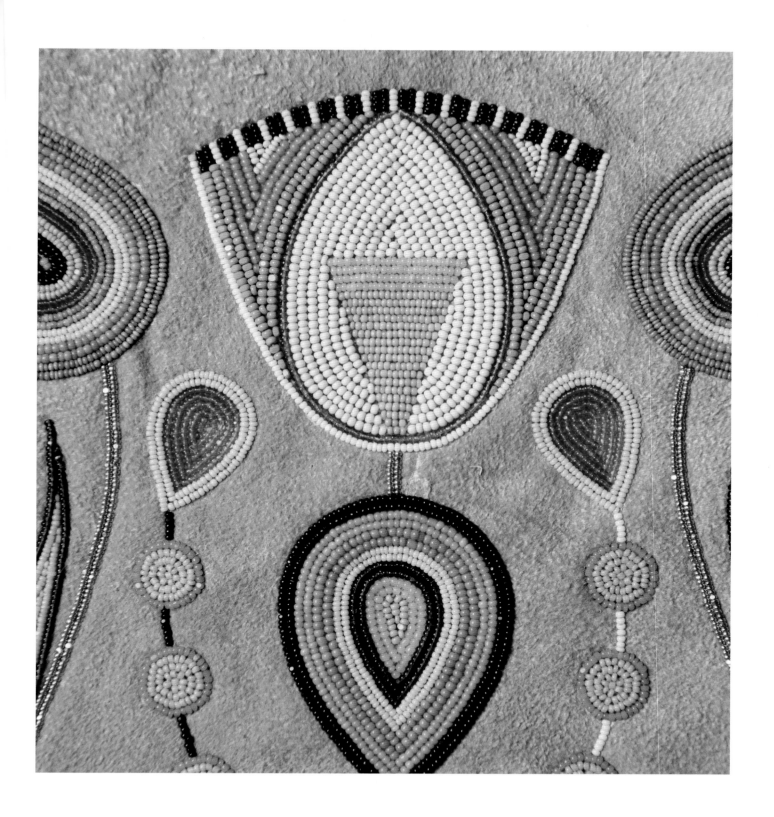

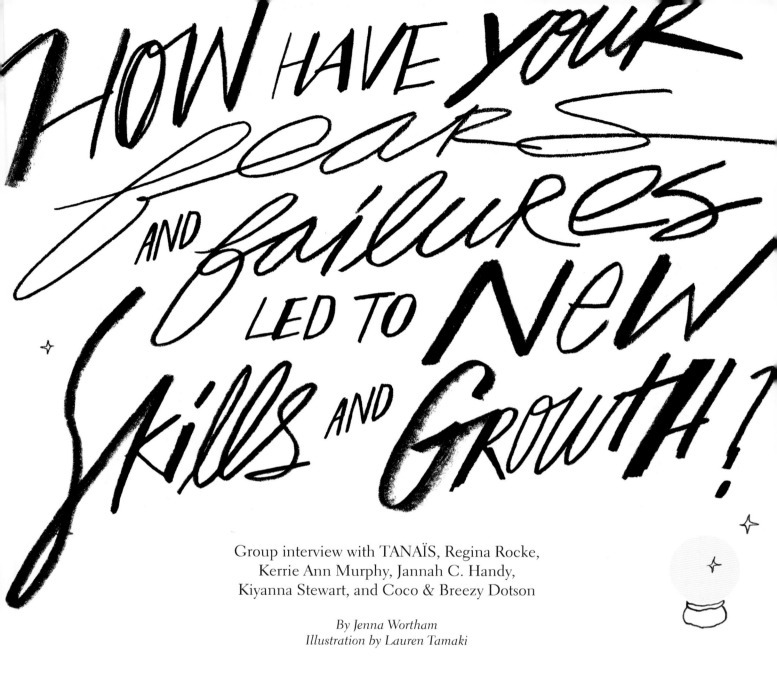

HOW HAVE YOUR FEARS AND FAILURES LED TO NEW SKILLS AND GROWTH?

Group interview with TANAÏS, Regina Rocke,
Kerrie Ann Murphy, Jannah C. Handy,
Kiyanna Stewart, and Coco & Breezy Dotson

By Jenna Wortham
Illustration by Lauren Tamaki

Fear is a tricky beast, a changeling creature that easily can be as crippling as it can be motivating. There are untold barriers to success—and some of the most disastrous challenges are the ones that come from within.

I talked to seven incredible entrepreneurs who inspire me with their determination, resiliency, and business acumen: TANAÏS of Hi Wildflower; healer Regina Rocke of Wolf Medicine Magic; Kerrie Ann Murphy, aka DJ Bearcat; Jannah C. Handy and Kiyanna Stewart, founders of BLK MKT Vintage; and Coco and Breezy Dotson of Coco and Breezy Eyewear. We discussed the fears they encounter and how they keep those fears from derailing their ambition and the larger dreams they have for their creative enterprises.

What is your relationship to fear?

TANAÏS: I work best when a certain tenor of fear is present. The kind where you're afraid of what might happen if you don't do something. I never want to let life pass me by without creating the art I wanted to create, even if this is a messy process.

Regina Rocke: Really and truly, the only thing I avoid and have deep fear around is going to the dentist! It's probably my number one fear, and I procrastinate as much as I can when it comes to making an appointment for getting my teeth cleaned.

Jannah C. Handy: Fear has always been my nearest and dearest frenemy: close enough to know all my weakness and prey on them with an endearing vitriol, yet retaining a strange ability to motivate me in spite of it.

Kiyanna Stewart: Fear and I are close—we go way back. However, I've evolved to a place where I try not to judge myself for experiencing it. I'm learning to love myself through it instead.

Kerrie Ann Murphy: I am learning that while certain fears in relation to instinct are necessary for survival, most of the time fear is your brain playing tricks on you.

Coco & Breezy Dotson: We've encountered many things that we fear—violence, loss, outsider status, bullying, financial uncertainty, and the reality that we had to grow and change in life and business—but we've always brought each other into our dialogue with fear. In that sense, fear has often been a three-part conversation, and we've been able to help each other respond. Fear can also be a friend—it can be an exciting voice at the table, because it can motivate and focus us.

How does your fear manifest in your daily life?

TANAÏS: As a writer, I fear writing about what we're all taught to keep silent; about my survivorship, trauma passed down through generations, the legacy of war. My consciousness as a feminist and my experience as a Bangladeshi woman raised in a Muslim family create great stakes in my work. I always fear not doing enough to illuminate our complexities—each of us holds many identities in ourselves.

Regina Rocke: I have some fears around disappointing yoga and barre students, but thankfully, I have to face those fears pretty much on a daily basis, so each week is a chance to confront that fear and grow from what I experience. I think sometimes students don't realize it, but a *lot* is projected onto yoga teachers. A lot is asked of us. Some people just show up to class, do the practice, say thanks, and leave, and that's it. Other times I'm a sounding board for a lot of turmoil and trauma that folks are going through. I'm happy to take this on, but when people are disappointed with how I show up for them as a teacher, that sometimes hurts, and I often fear that I'm disappointing certain students.

Jannah C. Handy: Fear shows up for me as questions; whether questioning my ability, my worth, or my superficial insecurities. It has manifested itself as creative blocks, half-started projects, and hours of some serious procrastination. Every day, fear asks me the same question: *Why would you think you are good/talented/intelligent/funny/innovative enough to . . . ?* A pseudo–impostor syndrome that forces me to second—and third—guess my natural creative instincts and skills that have gotten me to where I am today.

Kiyanna Stewart: Fear is always showing up and showing its ass. I've struggled with anxiety for many years and understand now that my fears are rooted in perfectionism. Fear manifests as bouts of self-doubt, impostor syndrome, and not listening to my gut. Those moments are mostly fleeting, but still impact me.

Kerrie Ann Murphy: There are different scales, but mostly in my career. What if I'm not booked enough this month, how will I make these ends meet? It also plays out in how ambitious I feel creatively—am I going to hide behind other people's music for the rest of my life, or will I eventually release my own?

Coco & Breezy Dotson: Fear often manifests itself as a kind of discomfort that we've learned to welcome, because it has been the precursor to a lot of positive changes, ideas, and adaptations. We've gotten more comfortable with it, because we've started to understand it as potential energy. With maturity and exposure to the world, we've become less fearful, as we've gotten a stronger sense of our values.

What routines/rituals/practices do you employ to keep fear at bay?

I work best when a certain tenor of fear is present. The kind where you're afraid of what might happen if you don't do something.

TANAÏS: My love taught me a Tibetan breathing meditation to usher in dreaming; I do this morning and night. I free dance each day. I journal each night to clear my mind of the day's thoughts. I don't eat meat anymore. I smoke herb to untether myself.

Regina Rocke: I always feel better after engaging in connecting to my body. I also think a lot about my spiritual teachings on lessons as movement toward growth. I try to see profound/triggering events as a teaching moment and what I am to have learned from these events. The problem with life and being in human form is that we are given tests with the lesson coming after. In formal school settings we are given lessons that hopefully prepare us for the test. In life, however, we are given the exam and then expected to just sort of come through with the lesson on our own. I have to sift through past experiences, continuing patterns, past relationships . . . all to hopefully arrive at the lesson that is meant to be learned. It really is insane, if you think about it.

Jannah C. Handy: Positive self-talk has been one of my saving graces when it comes to challenging fears. It allows me to change the inner (and sometimes outer) narrative that can convolute my drive/direction and make me doubt my abilities. A helpful mantra that I use is from my mother, by way of Yoda (yes, my mom is a Jedi Master, ahead of her time). She would say, "Be bold, and mighty forces will come to your aid."

Kiyanna Stewart: The most important practice that keeps me most free of fear and anxiety is articulating honest, hard truths and sharing them with others, even when it's challenging. I consider Audre Lorde to be not only my literary mother, but also a spiritual mother, and her opening line of "The Transformation of Silence into Language and Action" is one of the most profound expressions I've ever heard. So much so that I had it tattooed down my spine. She writes, "I have come to believe over and over again that what is most important to me must be spoken, made verbal and shared, even at the risk of having it bruised or misunderstood. That the speaking profits me, beyond any other effect." This sentiment grounds me and keeps me honest and fearless, in spite of conflict, tension, and the unknown. I'm also a fan of deep-breathing exercises—particularly outdoors.

Kerrie Ann Murphy: Physical exertion and stretching are good ones for me. I can feel the anxiety, fear, and toxins draining out of my body. I smoke a lot of weed and burn a lot of candles.

Coco & Breezy Dotson: It seems simple, but we try to talk about the issues creating the fear. That doesn't always mean dissecting the fear itself—it's possible to give the emotion too much attention. We also emphasize keeping the rest of our lives balanced to better handle challenges. Eating well, exercising, meditating, and taking time for ourselves and with loved ones are all important aspects of how we handle fear.

Nina Simone, while talking about what freedom means to her, says that it's a feeling that is "no fear." What does that iteration of freedom—having no fear—look like to you?

TANAÏS: When I don't feel fear, it means I am finally trusting the process. I'm letting a situation take the time it takes.

Regina Rocke: What I think of first is coming into a place of really and truly understanding that everything is being provided for me. There is no lack. Wanting—desire—is said to be the root of all suffering, and until we let go, surrender, and let the universe provide, we will not experience true joy and freedom. Freedom from desire leads to freedom, in my opinion.

Jannah C. Handy: Fear operates as your brain's fail-safe to stop you from doing something "stupid," technically speaking. Freedom as "no fear" is the ability to move throughout this world with your heart as your compass, unencumbered by the thoughts, fears, or rationale of the brain.

Kiyanna Stewart: This looks like living my life with an ethic of unapologetic honesty to myself and to others. If I allow fear to control and guide my decision-making, am I moving as my most authentic self? Am I really free? No.

Kerrie Ann Murphy: Challenging it, which is a very mindful and personal practice. I am very much with the warrior mind-set of "no fear." I think that looks like a lot of confidence, which is a message I support.

Coco & Breezy Dotson: It's easy to be caught making decisions reactively, and you need to find the space to think into the future without day-to-day fears clouding your vision. (For example, we've certainly signed a few contracts over the years that helped us avoid the fear of economic uncertainty but distracted from our broader strategy.) There can be a freedom *in* fear. Fear can engage and focus you; when you force yourself to jump, you don't have time for doubts. Fear has often given us the freedom of a fierce attention to what we wanted.

The philosopher Thich Nhat Hanh says, "We have the power to look deeply at our fears, and then fear cannot control us." What fears have you looked at deeply recently, and did that looking deconstruct their power?

TANAÏS: For the first time, I'm thinking of aging. What it feels like to age as a woman. It's partly a fear of my body or face aging, or even dying; it's also this fear of not delv-

ing in deep enough to create work that expresses my personal and political and emotional landscape.

Regina Rocke: I was really in a place of scarcity for a long, long time. There was a reality to it. I really and truly was barely scraping by financially, but also, there was a lot of imagined lack involved, too. I started to shift my thinking around abundance and also got very focused about advancing my career, and it has paid off. I'm doing what I love, and it's paying the bills, and I'm still moving forward toward bigger goals.

Jannah C. Handy: One of my biggest fears is death. The finality and eternal nature of it can send me into a fear-spiral about something I clearly have no control over. I cannot let the fear of the inevitable paralyze me. I began to examine what was at the root of my fear of death and decided to sit in the fear and take inventory of what the actual fears were of: having unfinished business, missing important moments in my daughter's life. The idea of my demise—*sorry, being dramatic*—started to become more manageable, as I live a bold life for as long as I am fortunate to do so.

Kiyanna Stewart: Lately I've been ruminating over the visibility that comes with social media and digitally mediated communities. As my business BLK MKT Vintage grows and becomes more visible, so do I and my partner. Looking deeply at these fears of "messing it up," "doing it all wrong," and not being able to live up to folks' expectations has subverted their powers and made me feel powerful—mostly

The most important practice that keeps me most free of fear and anxiety is articulating honest, hard truths and sharing them with others, even when it's challenging.

because I was just being brave, honest, and courageous in doing so. Instead of judging myself for having these fears, I'm recognizing that they're a natural part of the entrepreneurial journey and will wax/wane.

Kerrie Ann Murphy: I have survived three near-death experiences, and the PTSD resulted in extreme anxiety that I could die at any given moment, which is, of course, true, but not where my mind needed to be focused. Circling back around to the brain playing tricks—this is exactly what was playing out for me. I am not really exactly sure what made this feeling fade away, but it did—maybe the sheer guarantee and the work I have done toward a better outlook, but I have learned to accept the inevitable.

Coco & Breezy Dotson: The difference between not wanting to do something and fear isn't always clear. Sometimes, we'll think we're against doing something, like asking for help or taking a risk, only to discover that taking that step actually makes sense and that it's fear holding us back. For example, we've begun to realize that asking for things is important but often remain scared to make an ask. With that in mind, we've been working on starting small, practicing minor acts of delegating to colleagues or asserting ourselves in public spaces on simple issues about, for example, manners. **gc**

Desiree Akhavan

Director, producer, and actress Desiree Akhavan on the importance of telling stories that haven't been told before.

By Fariha Roísín
Photography by Rebecca Naen

Desiree Akhavan is the kind of director who, when I first watched her film *Appropriate Behaviour*, back in 2014, I felt a kinship with I rarely feel when watching the plethora of American films that seem to perpetuate the same message. Whether it's the recycling of the same white family, with similar but negligible differences, or the white women we are told to desire, admire, and envy, there is a script. Akhavan herself knows this script—the hollow reproduction of film for a supposed (white, cis, straight) market, but rarely for a purpose—and she distinctly makes art outside of it. In fact, her style is so unique in its storytelling that it resonates with a force, like great art often does, to an audience (like me) who so desperately needs it.

Appropriate Behaviour, similar to Cheryl Dunye's *The Watermelon Woman*, left me feeling seen in a sexuality discourse, by a woman of color, that we *really* lack, i.e., the complexities of identifying as queer, or bisexual, and how the way people see or sometimes *refuse* to see you can be challenging, as well as frustrating. Janelle Monáe may have just come out as pansexual after years of circling around the question of her sexuality, but biphobia still exists, and there are many important conversations yet to be had. This is why representation is so vital; as humans we are so complex that just one system, or one story (or even a few), isn't enough to affirm us of our definitions.

Most recently Akhavan premiered her latest film, *The Miseducation of Cameron Post*, at Sundance, where she won the Grand Jury Prize. The film stars Chloë Grace Moretz, Sasha Lane, and Forrest Goodluck as three kids sent to a Christian "de-gaying" camp. It's a harrowing story that describes the tortures of being gay (and also non-binary/trans), and yet there are so many subtle moments of care and concern in the film, reminding me that community—and your chosen family—are sometimes the most important facets of both your survival and your personhood. We owe a lot to these people in our lives, and it's beautiful. Despite the brief moments of absolute trauma, it's largely a story about togetherness, and how we support and protect one another. The end is hopeful: It's about a beginning.

Recently, I got a chance to talk to Akhavan, her in London, working on her latest project—*The Bisexual*, for UK's

Post made everyone's life easier, but then I put myself in *The Bisexual*. They know who I am by now.

In *Appropriate Behaviour*, despite inevitably having your character's mother, Nasrin (who was played by Anh Duong!), dismissing you when you say, "I'm a little gay," the family itself is portrayed as being quite close, and familial, despite their differences. How have your own (Iranian) parents interacted with your queerness?

We had to go through an adjustment period, but we got through it, and they could not be more supportive, and through this experience I've gotten to know what unconditional love is, having tested it. I wish I could tell my younger self to have more patience, more faith, and to know that coming out takes bravery/courage on both sides, not just mine.

Iran has a strong history and legacy of art, are there things that inspire you from that culture?

Kourosh Yaghmaei's *Back from the Brink*.

What advice would you give to young brown kids, young queer kids, who are looking up to you and wanting to make films?

Make things. Do not wait for other people to enable you. You don't need money or connections to make things. Don't worry about looking stupid. Whatever you do, you will look stupid, and nobody will care

as much as you do. Trust your instincts. Don't get into bed with someone bigger than you, especially at first—work with people who are as invested as you are. Don't worry about following the rules—make up your own rules.

Tell me about winning the Grand Jury Prize at Sundance. What was that like?

It was like any accomplishment. Acing the test, getting the job, finding out your crush likes you back: an instant burst of joy followed by a chorus of insecurities diminishing the accomplishment until you're convinced it's not really that big a deal. Then you come up with a laundry list of goals you haven't achieved and decide that once you achieve those, you can allow yourself to feel like a fully formed, successful human.

In your prerecorded speech you mentioned, "I was raised on film and television, it was a third parent to me, but I grew up always wishing that that parent resembled me a little bit more, and I'm hoping that with this film we made something that speaks to the people you don't usually hear about on-screen." What does representation look like to you?

It feels like mainstream cinema operates under the assumption that there's one way to be alive. One color, one sexuality, one morality, one way to be a woman, one way to be a man and we all allowed ourselves

to be taken along for that ride. I want films that don't regurgitate the same stories and shots and bodies and perspectives. Films where there's more than one way to interpret a situation. Filmmakers who have more faith in their audience and the balls to put something honest/personal and potentially ugly out there.

What inspires you?

I'm inspired by new approaches to standard forms of entertainment (*Black Panther*), people talking openly and honestly about taboo or too-personal subject matter (*The Argonauts* by Maggie Nelson, *The Rules Do Not Apply* by Ariel Levy), making the political personal (*120 BMP*), absurd comedy that pokes fun at art and morality (*Force Majeure* and *The Square*), open, frank discussion about sex and power (Catherine Breillat, *Slutever*).

It's depressing that all my inspiration comes from the world of film/literature/TV, and I would love to be able to reference kindness, bravery, and intelligence outside of art, but I've limited my life to consuming and creating this shit and in that way I'm only half formed, which is why it's bullshit that I'm sharing my thoughts/ideas/influences publicly.

I feel like oftentimes there's such a fetishization of queerness that focuses on our grief, but there was something so hopeful about The Miseducation of Cameron Post. Is that something you were aware of when you were making it?

Yes. It was always a teen coming-of-age film. We didn't want these kids feeling victimized or different from you and your friends—it would keep the horror of what happens to them at arm's length. I've always found that the most traumatic episodes of my life have been laced in joy/hope and humor. **gc**

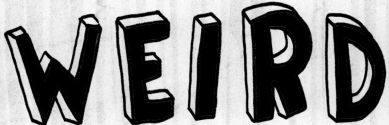

HOW TO COLLABORATE WITH FRIENDS ON CREATIVE PROJECTS *without* MAKING THINGS WEIRD

written by: LORA DiFRANCO

illustrated by: KATIE DAUGHERTY

MIXING *FRIENDSHIP* AND BUSINESS CAN BE A TRICKY THING. BUT... *IT'S ALL I DO.*

AS THE FOUNDER OF FREE PERIOD PRESS, I COLLABORATE WITH DIFFERENT ARTISTS & DESIGNERS TO CREATE CUTE PAPER THINGS TO HELP FOLKS *slow down*, REFLECT, AND FOCUS ON WHAT'S **IMPORTANT.**

I STARTED FREE PERIOD PRESS BECAUSE I HAD A **LONG** LIST OF PRODUCTS THAT I WANTED TO SEE IN THE WORLD. SINCE I HAVE **ZERO** DESIGN SKILLS, I TURNED TO MY VERY TALENTED ARTIST FRIENDS TO HELP BRING THEM TO *life.*

AND FOR THE MOST PART, THIS SETUP HAS BEEN <u>AMAZING!</u> I'M OFTEN BLOWN AWAY WITH HOW A DESIGNER CAN TAKE MY **ORIGINAL** IDEA AND ADD THEIR OWN *twist* TO THE PROJECT, MAKING THE FINAL PRODUCT **SO MUCH BETTER** THAN WHAT I ORIGINALLY HAD IN MIND.

However, WORKING WITH FRIENDS BRINGS A **VERY SPECIFIC** SET OF CHALLENGES AND I WAS DEFINITELY BLINDSIDED BY THEM WHEN I FIRST STARTED.

BETTER TOGETHER!

Story time:

OUR FIRST PRODUCT WAS A COLORING BOOK, EXCEPT (wait for it) IT WAS FOR **ADULTS**. IT WAS A NOVEL IDEA AT THE TIME, <u>I SWEAR</u>. MY FRIENDS ERIN, ALI & JOE KINDLY AGREED TO CONTRIBUTE PATTERNED PAGES.

THE PROCESS WAS A BUMPY RIDE *to say the least*. I WAS SO UNCOMFORTABLE **OWNING MY OWN IDEA** THAT MY FRIENDS WERE LEFT WITH AMBIGUOUS DIRECTION, NOT KNOWING <u>WHAT</u> TO MAKE OR <u>HOW</u> TO MAKE IT.

WE MADE IT TO THE FINISH LINE WITH A GREAT COLORING BOOK AND OUR *friendship* INTACT, BUT I WALKED AWAY WITH SOME **KEY** LESSONS ABOUT HOW TO CO-CREATE WITH FRIENDS.

LOOKING BACK, I REALIZED THAT:

* I WAS **SUPER** ATTACHED TO MY ORIGINAL IDEA & WAS RELUCTANT TO LET IT *evolve*.

* I HAD A **SPECIFIC** VISION, BUT LACKED CONFIDENCE TO COMMUNICATE IT CLEARLY.

* I <u>ASSUMED</u> MY FRIENDS WOULD TAKE OWNERSHIP OF THE IDEA & RUN WITH IT, INSTEAD OF LOOKING *to me* FOR GUIDANCE.

* I WASN'T USED TO TELLING PEOPLE **WHAT TO DO**. AND THESE WERE MY *friends*, SO I DIDN'T WANT TO DO ANYTHING THAT WOULD POTENTIALLY **UPSET** THEM! (YOU STILL LIKE ME RIGHT???)

IN MY ATTEMPT TO BE A *likeable, laid-back collaborator*, MY FRIENDS WERE LEFT WITHOUT CLEAR DIRECTION AND TIMELINES, AND I WAS LEFT WONDERING WHY THE PROJECT WASN'T MOVING ALONG FASTER.

SINCE THAT FIRST PROJECT, I'VE LAUNCHED SEVERAL OTHER PRODUCTS WITH DIFFERENT FRIENDS, AND I'VE LEARNED **SO MUCH** ABOUT HOW TO MAKE A COLLABORATION WORK FOR EVERYONE INVOLVED. I HOPE THIS GUIDE (SEE NEXT PAGE) WILL HELP YOU CREATE **AMAZING** THINGS WITH YOUR FRIENDS WHILE KEEPING EVERYONE ON THE **SAME PAGE.**

ME THEN:

I DUNNO! WHATEVER YOU GUYS THINK!! I DON'T KNOW ANYTHING! LOLOLOL

ME NOW:

LET'S CREATE A MUTUALLY BENEFICIAL AGREEMENT THAT **CLEARLY DEFINES** OUR EXPECTATIONS OF EACH OTHER!

A GUIDE TO COLLABORATING WITH PALS

Here are some questions to consider as you get ready to work with friends.

WHERE ARE YOU ON THIS SCALE?

I have a VAGUE idea of what I want the final product to be.

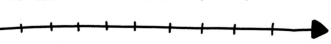

I know EXACTLY what I want, complete with Pinterest board, mockups, and specifications of the final product.

WHAT, exactly, IS YOUR IDEA?

_____
_____
_____

WHAT ARE YOU SUPER CLEAR ABOUT?

_____
_____
_____

WHAT IS OPEN TO INTERPRETATION?

_____
_____
_____

 WHAT IS YOUR TIMELINE?

_____

WHO IS GOING TO *Own* THE FINAL PRODUCT?

_____

WHO IS GOING TO *market* IT?

_____

HOW MUCH CAN YOU *pay* YOUR COLLABORATORS?
(The answer should NEVER be "*exposure*" ☞☞) IS IT A ONE-TIME PAYMENT,
OR DO THEY GET A CUT OF THE PRODUCT'S SALES?

_____

PRO TIPS

FOR THE MOST PART, **NO ONE IS GOING TO CARE ABOUT YOUR PROJECT AS MUCH AS YOU CARE ABOUT YOUR PROJECT.**

SURE, YOUR FRIENDS WANT TO DO A GOOD JOB, BUT THEY ARE PROBABLY NOT GOING TO LOSE SLEEP OVER THE PROJECT LIKE YOU ARE. (NOT THAT YOU'LL BE LOSING SLEEP. YOU ARE A COOL, CALM, AND COLLECTED ENTREPRENEUR WITH *nothing but confidence* THAT EVERYTHING WILL TURN OUT GREAT... *OBVIOUSLY.*)

CRITIQUING EACH OTHER'S WORK DOES NOT MEAN YOU'RE CRITIQUING EACH OTHER AS A **PERSON.** YOU'RE JUST TRYING TO MAKE THE PRODUCT THE BEST IT CAN BE. **FRAME YOUR FEEDBACK CONSTRUCTIVELY** AND IN TERMS OF YOUR VISION OF THE PROJECT. (EXAMPLE: *"This feels more formal than I was looking for."* INSTEAD OF *"This doesn't feel right."*)

STAY OPEN-MINDED

TO INTERPRETATIONS OF YOUR IDEA. ALLOW IT TO GROW & EVOLVE WHILE KEEPING YOUR TARGET AUDIENCE IN MIND. WHAT WILL SERVE THEM BEST? (AND DON'T BE AFRAID TO ASK YOUR AUDIENCE ALONG THE WAY IF YOU NEED A FRESH PERSPECTIVE.)

AFTER YOU'VE AGREED ON THE TERMS OF YOUR COLLABORATION, **PUT IT IN WRITING!** IT DOESN'T HAVE TO BE AN OVERLY COMPLICATED LEGAL DOCUMENT, BUT A SHORT AGREEMENT MAKES SURE THAT EVERYONE IS ON THE *same page.*

THERE MAY ALWAYS BE SOME INHERENT AWKWARDNESS WHEN YOU'RE WORKING WITH FRIENDS (ESPECIALLY IF YOU'RE A PEOPLE-PLEASER LIKE I AM), BUT... YOU KNOW, **LIFE IS AWKWARD! DO IT ANYWAY!**

IT'S TOTALLY WORTH IT!!!

REVO LUT ION BOOT CAMP

Meet the women changing the face of angel investing and creating capital for women and non-binary femme social entrepreneurs.

By Meg José Mateo
Photography by Kelly Marshall

It's been two days since Natalia Oberti Noguera wrapped Pipeline Angels' Spring 2018 Pitch Summit, a three-week, seven-city tour from Boston to Seattle and ending in Minneapolis. The thirty-four-year-old cis-queer Latina founder and CEO is still on a high, even as she's back in the Brooklyn apartment she shares with her partner, Chuin Lee. "I'm passionate about activating local capital for local entrepreneurs," she says. "Next we're planning to launch our signature angel-investing boot camp in San Juan, Puerto Rico, to support the island's founders and economy."

Since its inception in 2011, Pipeline Angels has been helping women- and femme-led, for-profit social ventures secure funding. In its portfolio, it boasts businesses ranging from Mented, a beauty line directed at women of color, to Thurst, a dating app for queer people of any gender. "According to the #ProjectDiane report, Black women start-up founders raise $36,000 on average, while the average, mostly white-male-led, *failed* start-up raises $1.3 million," Natalia points out.

Trouble raising funds was a common grievance among the early members of New York Women Social Entrepreneurs (NYWSE), a group Natalia started in 2008 and grew from just six women to over 1,200 in just two years. These women's experiences often followed a similar storyline: They went around to their networks getting people excited about their change-making ideas, and people would validate them by saying, "Let me know where to send the check." But as soon as the women clarified that it was a for-profit

MORGEN BROMELL

Founder of Thurst (thurst.co), a dating
app for queer people of any gender.

SASKIA SORROSA

Founder of Fresh Bellies (freshbellies.com),
a platform with a mission to create a new
generation of healthful adventurous eaters.

social venture, these would-be supporters backed away, saying, "Let me know when you start your sister nonprofit." These stories left an indelible impression on Natalia. "I realized that society has a gendered perception on how we can change the world. If a woman or femme says they're going to change the world, society thinks they're going to launch a nonprofit. If a guy says he's going to change the world, they're *not*

thinking he's going to launch a nonprofit," she says.

Her solution to this fund-raising problem: Show women and femmes how to become angel investors who invest in women- and femme-led businesses. At Pipeline Angels, members participate in a four-month-long boot camp that teaches them the secrets of angel investing. For a fee of $4,500 and an investment minimum of $5,000, members

attend workshops on topics such as due diligence and values, which are led by experts, including seasoned angel investors, VCs, and impact investing professionals. At the end of the program, the cohort chooses a company to invest in from one of the Pitch Summit participants. In return, they receive equity in the company. "So many high-net-worth women and femmes often make a positive impact with their money through charitable

BRITTANY FINKLE

Founder of the rentable bridal
accessories platform, Happily Ever
Borrowed (happilyeverborrowed.com).

NATALIA OBERTI NOGUERA

Founder and CEO of Pipeline
Angels (pipelineangels.com).

donations," Natalia explains. "I wanted to create a bridge from philanthropy to angel investing, and share with them that they can make a positive impact with their money by investing in women- and femme-led for-profit social ventures."

Natalia's ambitious agenda is summed up on T-shirts given to members at boot camp: *I'm Changing the Face of Angel Investing*. And this bold statement is something

she means literally, as the field of angel investing is overwhelmingly white and male. "It's important for me to create visible examples of women and femmes who are 'sharks,'" she says (with a reference to the nickname for the investors on the television show *Shark Tank*).

Natalia was born in Bogota, Colombia, but moved around a lot growing up. In fact, at about two weeks of age she

relocated to New Jersey, where her Colombian mother and Italian father were based. Because of her father's peripatetic career working for the UN, she spent long spells of her childhood in Ecuador, Colombia, and Honduras, and her teenage years in the Dominican Republic, where she finished high school. "Moving around has made me resilient," she remarks. "One of the best skills an entrepreneur can have is

TANYA VAN COURT

Founder of Goalsetter (goalsetter.co), a platform that transforms gift-giving into goal-giving.

better sense of who I was, which, it turns out, includes being queer." It was at this internship at Net Impact that she learned about sustainable business practices and social entrepreneurism.

While Natalia says that entrepreneurship has its challenges, she's grateful that it's allowed her to have less fear, particularly with regard to discrimination in the workplace for being queer. "Entrepreneurship can be hard. It also means that I'm my own boss, and this has made me more committed to being out and being vocal about it. I don't have to worry about getting fired or potentially missing out on a promotion for being queer. Unfortunately, there are still a lot of people in 2018 who still have that reasonable fear. In fact, there are some US states that don't have protections regarding workplace discrimination. Creating a culture where people can feel comfortable bringing their full selves to work is really important to me."

Natalia is determinedly upbeat about securing a future for women and femme social entrepreneurs. Over the last seven years, Pipeline Angels has had more than three hundred members graduate from their angel-investing boot camp. Members have invested more than $5 million in more than fifty companies through their Pitch Summit program. And the NYWSE celebrated its ten-year anniversary in April 2018, with one of the Pipeline Angels' members, Kerry Ann Rockquemore, speaking at the event. "Being a leader means bringing people into the room and bringing more voices to the table." Natalia smiles. "When you do that, you create something bigger, you create a movement." gc

adaptability. As a kid, I didn't realize it was a skill I was learning—it's something I use day in and day out."

She would continue moving, attending Yale in 2001 as an undergrad student. "While I doubled in comparative literature and economics, I like to say that I majored in extracurriculars," she quips. In 2006 Natalia relocated to Milan to attend a master's program in international

healthcare management, economics, and policy at SDA Bocconi. She was interested in living in Italy, and it also allowed her to be closer to her younger sister, who was attending a nearby university. After Milan, she headed to San Francisco to fulfill a required internship for her master's program. "Milan was too close to the Vatican for comfort." She laughs. "And San Francisco was a better place to be, as I was getting a

Success Stories

MENTED

Six years ago, Kristen Jones Miller, thirty-one, and Amanda Johnson, thirty-two, met during their first year at Harvard Business School. The two quickly became friends. In March 2017, their friendship transformed into a business venture when they launched Mented—short for pigmented—a makeup brand featuring vegan, nontoxic products formulated for women of color. It all started after Miller and Johnson commiserated on the difficulty to find a nude lip color for their skin tone. "We started Mented because we believe every woman should be able to find herself in the world of beauty," says Miller. Later in 2017, at the Pipeline Angels Pitch Summit, they secured $75,000 in funding which helped them to scale their marketing efforts. "It was great being in a room full of women, which almost never happens in a pitch," says Miller.

BEAUTYLYNK

Boston native Rica Elysée, thirty-two, wanted to create opportunities for stylists focusing on Black women's beauty services, as well as those that specialize in a variety of hair textures. Her app BeautyLynk connects busy clients in need of services with traveling beauty professionals. Since launching in 2015, the app offers more than 10,000 stylists covering thirty-two markets including four key markets in Atlanta, Boston, Washington, DC, and Philadelphia. The growth came in part from an investment from Pipeline Angels. "It was a great opportunity to connect to female investors," says Elysée, "I've learned lots about scaling and building a company from them."

HAPPILY EVER BORROWED

In 2011, Brittany Finkle was just twenty-three when she started Happily Ever Borrowed. A graduate of the Fiber Science Apparel Design program at Cornell, she had been helping one of her sisters plan her wedding when she realized just how expensive the dress and accessories were, especially for a single day's use. Her solution: a luxury, e-boutique that rents bridal accessories including tiaras, belts, and jewelry. She attended Pipeline Angel's Pitch Summit in 2012 and received $10,000 that allowed her to invest in more inventory and test some marketing in the early stages. "It was one of my first 'real' pitch summits," says Finkle. "I remember feeling incredibly nervous and intimidated by the other groups pitching as I felt my company had less 'social good' compared to some other groups. But in the end, I believed in sustainability, eliminating waste in the fashion industry, and helping women spend less money on their wedding day."

A Fear of Starting Over

Reflections on the Sophomore Slump

By TANAÏS
Photography by Jessica Antola

Fiction ushers us closer to understanding our human experience. I write from multitudes—as a woman, queer, femme, Bengali, Muslim—and resist being labeled as one identity. Being a writer is not quite a stable career path, but it is a privilege to be able to use written language to tell stories. For the decade I worked on my novel *Bright Lines*, a coming-of-age story centered on a Bangladeshi Muslim family in Brooklyn, I reminded myself of this privilege. I wrote comfortably from a place of relative obscurity. No one knew me, and I had the freedom to write what I pleased. Yet when I finally published my novel and toured the country, I fell hard into a yearlong depression. I blamed my travel diet of French fries and Moscow Mules. I blamed the election. I blamed the New York City winter, even though these are ideal conditions for locking yourself inside and writing away the snow day.

New fears emerged, on opposite poles: I feared that my sophomore effort would neither live up to my first book nor transcend my debut. Starting the process all over felt like learning to crawl again. The sheer thought of writing myself down the wrong path blocked me from getting on the path. I couldn't bear the thought of writing hundreds of manuscript pages, knowing subconsciously that they'd never see the light of day. There were infinite variations of the story I wanted to tell. How would I find the right one?

Along with these concerns, I had to think about how I'd find enough time to write when I had to run my business. Hi

Wildflower, the independent beauty and fragrance house I started in 2014, is my day job. I started this brand after a two-year stint unemployed, and just as it started to grow, I published my book. I started the brand after getting laid off from a trendy (and, ultimately, failed) Brooklyn start-up. During my stint there, I had to swallow working for a mediocre, egomaniacal man, but I learned innumerable skills, like graphic design, marketing, branding, and product development, and most important, it's where I took my first perfume-blending class. With my weekly unemployment check, I slowly began to build an olfactory library of hundreds of essential oils and aroma chemicals to make perfume and candles. Frugality is not my strongest suit.

This early investment set me on a whole new path as an independent brand owner. Before I knew it, I started to get regular wholesale accounts for Hi Wildflower, and found myself growing the business exponentially just as my novel published. I went from having no job to having two jobs that required every part of my being. The disconnection between my physical body and the psychic terrain of my book stole my confidence to start the project. I tried to send new work to new agents, but each meeting ended with, "Come back when you're finished." I left the meetings feeling like I'd worked so hard to climb the impossible mountain of publishing a novel, and somehow I'd slipped and fallen back down to base camp.

When I travel alone, my fear of limitation dissolves, and I relearn what it means to be independent and navigate the unknown.

It dawned on me in therapy: I was depressed. My fear of the sophomore slump had grown so intense, it paralyzed my writing process. I described my new book: a novel about a woman encountering an artificial intelligence built and based on her late mother. "I can't seem to get inside this book," I said. "I know what it's about, but I don't feel smart enough to write this."

"Conceptually, I understand this," said Isabel, the therapist I've seen for the last ten years. We have worked through a lot of my relationship issues, stemming from an abusive relationship in high school and guilt around writing about explicit themes that would offend or disappoint my parents.

"But where are you in this story? How is it yours?"

"I feel pigeonholed, like I need to represent Bangladesh all the time. But I want to write something surreal, something not so tied to my lived experience and familial history," I said, finally articulating the root cause of my slump.

"Do you think you can write something surreal but that comes from the richness of your experience?"

"Shit, I don't know. Not if I can't find the damn time to write." For months, my despair sharpened into anger and frustration without much provocation. This unsettled me, made it harder to sit in my thoughts.

"Can you make time to write in the morning each day?"

"I'm not a morning person," I cried. I was no stranger to watching the sunrise because I hadn't slept.

"You need a ritual, something you can do each day just for yourself."

Rituals are the reason I created Hi Wildflower, but I'd gotten so immersed in the grind that I couldn't remember the last time I'd actually lit a candle in my house and lay back to relax. I had too much on my mind, at all times. It wasn't until I threw my neck out from cleaning the studio that I needed a drastic change. My acupuncturist suggested that I start free dancing to my favorite music to move my energy throughout my body. My approach to healing has always been holistic, and this seemed like a simple way to get some exercise and generate joy.

This first step opened a new door for my writing process—I had a bit more energy and clarity, but still, I couldn't write. I knew that my day-to-day business matters stole the stillness and quietude I needed to work on the novel. I had to take a risk I wasn't quite sure I could afford, thus learning the hard lesson that every entrepreneur faces: Without sacrifice, there is no reward. For years, I'd bootstrapped my operation, but in a business, sacrifice often means shelling out money—that you don't necessarily have—to expand your vision. There was no way I could toil in the studio each day to physically pour candles, make perfume,

ship goods to customers, and handle operations, sales, and production and write a novel. I was caught in the no-man's-land of working 24/7 on my small business and lamenting the novel I wanted to write but could not seem to find the time to.

Once I made the leap to outsource labor, shipping, and production—for debt is a rite of passage to profit—the rest of the doors opened.

As conducive to solitude as a New York winter is, the lack of vitamin D does take its toll on all the city's denizens. After six months of working to automate my business operations and slowly introducing ritual back into my life through daily journaling, breath meditation, and dance, I was ready for a ritual I could embark on each year, every March: a feminist solo travel into nature.

When I travel alone, my fear of limitation dissolves, and I relearn what it means to be independent and navigate the unknown. I know that the first few days of the trip will send me into a spiral, a withdrawal from my day-to-day life. This is not a vacation, after all. *My business has afforded me this freedom, this is a privilege that I must not waste*, I tell myself. The immensity of the task overwhelms me, and I focus on small things, like buying groceries to make a large pot of soup so that I don't have to cook for days. I know I've carved out this space to think and write, but I can't start until I've released a long, drawn-out cry.

For the last two years, my yearly sojourn

has taken me to California's high desert. I never experienced the desert as a young girl; my family lived in the Midwest, and the farthest we ventured was the Rockies. The desert is a space of infinite metaphor. As I contemplate the void, I witness life, everywhere, crawling, scurrying, buzzing in the sand and sun-dried flora. I see my brown skin in the colors of the sand. I alternate between staring at the sun and its inverted negative, glowing on the empty page of my journal. Each day, I choose a new boulder, weathered by eons, to sit on, and write by hand until I lose the sun and sit in shadows. Several days pass in this still sameness. I write sentence by sentence, collecting them into pages, like catching rainwater in my palms. After several days, I start to transcribe my scribbles onto the computer, which feels less cold. When the day's writing is done, I drive back to the boulders as sunset surrenders to the stars. I only hear the sound of my breathing and the wind, and I reflect on how I got here. Fiction attempts to compress the infinite within the bounds of the author's imagination, and my book, like all works of art, is just another speck in the cosmic vastness. 𝓰𝓬

A Seat at the Table

An Interview with Shakirah Simley

By Ebony Haight
Photography by Maria Del Rio

Shakirah Simley is a young, Black woman hungry for change. She's dedicating herself to changing the future of food by empowering vulnerable communities, women, and youth. Shakirah is a community organizer, educator, and writer who has already spent over a decade working on food equity and policy issues.

For over five years, she led community outreach and strategy, youth development, and philanthropy programs as the community programs director and Canner-in-Residence for Bi-Rite, an iconic, independently owned family of sustainable food businesses in San Francisco. In 2016, she cofounded an organizing collaborative of people of color working in good food called Nourish|Resist. In its first six weeks, Nourish|Resist provided over 225 youth and local community members with capacity-building activities and direct-action education over delicious, lovingly made meals. We sat down with Shakirah over a glass of wine to learn more about the woman behind the work.

Which came first, the activism or the food?

Definitely the activism.

What are some of the earliest memories you have of seeing activism in action?

If you are doing well, you are always bringing your community up with you.

My grandmother Mini Imah Shabazz was a Black Panther, a fearless Muslim, and a social worker for domestic violence victims and people suffering with substance abuse. She was very well-known in our community. And my mother was also a social worker for people with substance abuse issues and for folks living with HIV and AIDS during the nineties in New York City. They laid the groundwork for me, and now I'm living their best dreams.

Growing up, my grandmother—in her beautiful headwrap and dashiki—was really particular about the kind of books that I had. The kind of dolls that I had. They all had to look like me. We always went to community celebrations. We always celebrated Kwanzaa. She was very strict, as far as our studies were concerned.

And with my mom, she was a single mom. She had me when she was fifteen, and raised five kids on her own. I graduated from college and she got her master's degree a week apart. She was very fierce, but more introverted. I remember while I was growing up, she worked for a nonprofit that was in Hell's Kitchen, and we would visit her clients. One week we would see that they were doing okay, and the next week we'd be taking out their belongings in a black trash bag because they had passed, with no family present.

And how old were you?

I was probably ten or eleven. They tried to protect us and make sure we grew up to be functioning adults, but they were also willing to expose us to life, to what was real. You know, we got sex ed real young. And in my family, we lost an aunt who was really dear to me to HIV and AIDS, and it was a conversation with my family in understanding how tough life is and how you need to keep going. And if you are doing well, you are always bringing your community up with you. You're never better than anybody else. Whatever you have can easily be taken away. Things are so precious.

I'm curious, what kind of food did you eat when you were growing up?

We had simple, easy carbs, whatever my mom could afford. There weren't any grocery stores in our neighborhood growing up, just bodegas with no apples or anything fresh. So we could just buy candy, tons of soda, and chips. Whenever we had fresh things, it was because my mom, when she worked on the Upper East Side or downtown, would stop at the fruit carts before getting on the train home. That's when we had cherries, or melon, or peaches. It was such a treat.

So we ate baked ziti. Franks and beans. Cube steak. Steak-umms—they're these frozen meat strips you can sauté and put in a sandwich. We ate whatever we could stretch and make do. That's how I learned to cook—for quantity, and based on hunger. Not for quality, pleasure, style, or technique. That came later.

When did you start to make that shift?

As a broke college student, you had to cook. It was cheaper to cook for myself than it was to eat at the dining hall. I didn't want to eat ramen all the time! I had been cooking for my family anyway, and knew how to stretch a dollar. I can look at a pretty bare pantry and work it out. And I had to do the same thing in college. So I was cooking for myself a lot, and I loved it.

With my tiny little bit of work-study money, I'd buy fresh pasta from the Amish farmers at the Clark Park Farmers' Market once a week. I was really intent on eating as well as I could based on the little bit of money that I had. And it was amazing. Just *so good*. So delicious. I'd never had that before.

How did you start to connect that new love of food with activism?

In college at Penn, where I spent four years trying to organize our on-campus security guards, I took a political science course called The Politics of Food and Opportunity. There had been times at Penn when I was really frustrated with the way communities of color had been pathologized in theory. I grew up in these communities. These "food deserts."

Well, I had a breakthrough in that course, which was all about hunger and the politics of hunger, and food access. I realized that when you talk about food, you can talk about race, class, gender, the economy,

housing, the workforce, immigration. I thought, *Maybe this is an opportunity for me to center my activism in a way that makes sense and is cohesive.*

So that seed was planted. Where did you go from there?

I ended up getting a fellowship with the New York City Commission on Human Rights; that was my first job after college. I also got involved with this organization called Just Food. They talked about food justice, which I hadn't heard about before. I'd heard about gender justice and social justice, but never food justice. And I was fascinated.

They trained me as a volunteer chef. I would go around to different neighborhoods, health fairs, or farmers' markets or church markets. Wherever they had a CSA drop-off, I would do a cooking demo. It was so cool. I just thought it was the best thing since sliced bread.

Did you have people who were touchpoints along the way? Who helped you out?

In college, I definitely had my second moms. Mentors who gave me a place to cry, were people who believed in me, provided safe spaces for me, or gave me a hot plate of food. They were so, so key. One of them was Valerie De Cruz; she was the executive director of Penn's Greenfield Intercultural Center. And a lot of my student

activism came through this center, which she supported.

I was the head of the United Minorities Council, representing the needs of students of color across campus. Being in these types of institutions, where you feel like it's a privilege for you to be there, you think, *I'm a scholarship kid, maybe I shouldn't be rocking the boat. I'm not supposed to be unionizing workers in one of the country's most powerful business schools. I'm not supposed to be taking on the department of public safety when they're racially profiling Black students as they're walking to class. I'm not supposed to be staging protests on campus.* I mean, I was definitely a troublemaker. But good trouble.

Okay, but so many people see that and they just kind of think, *That's not right,* then keep on doing their thing. But you are someone who *makes* it their thing. Why?

If not us, when? If not me, who? Somehow, I've been imbued with a sense of social responsibility and righteousness—which is not always the way to do things. And I guess I'm a little fearless. Or dumb. I don't know, maybe they go hand in hand.

I also think that's not a choice. Apathy is not an option. But I always try to come from a place of grace and empathy. Everybody has their own reasons why, or why not. You don't have to be involved—I'll still fight for you.

So what does a progressive future look like for you? If there were a successful conclusion to food equality, what would that look like?

Owning and controlling the means of our labor and production. Self-determination, so every person of color in this country has the right to reach their full potential and determine their own future. We can radically imagine what that future would look like if we include people. Not just include them, but have them at the head of the table, writing their own stories.

That future means a power shift. Some people are going to have to give things up in order to make room for others. It means you have more folks of color, more women, more queer people in positions of power. That applies to food, but it applies to all our systems. Our education system, our health system.

What I hear you saying is that for us to get the future you imagine, people will have to shift, as you once described it, from being allies to being accomplices. They will need to stop investigating what makes you so strong and start investigating where their own strength might come from.

Right. Because we've already lost so much. Think of all the Black potential that's been lost in this country since America was an idea. That is sobering. And, you know, people will ask me, "How are you so resilient?" I hate that question. It's not a choice. It's not a choice! It's not a choice. We are because we have to be. And that's fine. I don't hold that against anybody. That's life, and how I have to navigate it.

If you were to give some concise advice to the rest of us, something we could do to start pushing things in the right direction, what would you recommend?

Use your dinner table as a tool for revolution and resistance. Who's sitting around it? Who's coming into your home? Who are you having conversations with? A lot of activism has happened around kitchen tables. If you think about the civil rights movements, and Leah Chase's restaurant, a lot of plans for movements or marches happened within her walls, over her amazing food. I think we can do that today. Food is the great denominator. Everybody eats different things, but everybody eats. So we can start there, and then move the conversation. I think that's a starting place.

One of the things that's so compelling about your blending of the food world with activism is, I think, that most people are drawn to food because they like aesthetics—beautiful colors, nice smells, warm places—and that seems in such strong contrast to what activism typically looks like and maybe is really about.

Well, I do like those things. I studied in Italy, my palate is pretty refined. I can talk about wine and cheese and tell people how to properly taste olive oil, talk to you till I'm blue in the face about seasonality and what type of produce to use for what. I still have that food knowledge. But I want to share it in a way that's not pretentious. I can sit you down to this amazing artisan organic meal, and then say, "Let's talk about racial injustice." And that goes down a little bit easier. I think that can be really powerful.

What do you think of foodies? Do you identify as one?

I care about food, but I care way more about people. And I think that's where the food movement needs to go. We need to care about people first. If we focus on treating people better, food will be better. And everyone has their part to do, in whatever sphere they're in.

I was talking to Daniel Patterson, a friend and chef in San Francisco, the other day, and he said, "If you look at any of the prominent news organizations that have powerful restaurant reviewers, none of them are people of color, and most of them are men." Restaurants need those reviews in order to be financially successful. So if you have people ensuring the successful futures of people that look like them, how

I care about food, but I care way more about people. We need to care about people first. If we focus on treating people better, food will be better.

are women-of-color-owned food businesses going to be reviewed and uplifted on their merits and the other benefits they bring by presenting their business?

There's inequality not just in the production of food, but all its manifestations. It's been really rewarding to work with Julia [Turshen] and others on EATT (Equity at the Table), and break down those walls around representation. Our community is here, and we can find each other, and we can create our own resources if we need to.

Tell us more about what you're working on these days.

It's a little confusing for me! I'm at a stage where I'm going to continue to refine. I've always worked in food. This is just a different aspect. In my current job, I work for the San Francisco Public Utilities Commission (SFPUC), which does water, power, sewer. It's a really powerful agency with tremendous resources, which is why it's one of the few utility companies in the entire country that has a community benefits program. The whole point of that program is to make sure that our infrastructure positively impacts people and place. So wherever we are, if there's a way to make sure that we're uplifting community and place, we're going to do that work.

Some people think what I'm doing now is pretty different, but actually, it's not. I'm doing community and economic development work in a Black and brown community. And one of the first targeted areas that I can start with are food businesses. They're usually the anchors of communities.

What's your role at the SFPUC?

I stepped into a role as executive director of a large community center that the SFPUC owns and operates. That community center exists because of a historic environmental litigation that the PUC has with the Southeast community in San Francisco. Forty years ago, they built a huge sewer plant in the Bayview neighborhood—that sewer plant processes 80 percent of San Francisco's waste—in one of San Francisco's last Black neighborhoods.

Part of mitigating that impact is maintaining programs, educational resources, job training, green space, and childcare at this community center. And it's my job to make sure that the PUC delivers on that promise to this sector of the city.

What's the most challenging thing you've got on your plate?

Right now, I'm running the old community center and we're in the process of building a new one. I'm learning a lot about land use, zoning, politics, and community and economic development in San Francisco. It is really hard. But I feel like I'm supposed to be doing this. And I hope one day that in learning all this work, I'll be able to represent San Franciscans and maybe run for office. I don't know in what way, in what capacity. I haven't decided that yet. But I want to do the work. Because I feel like, when you have a person like me, with my background, actually being able to represent folks, then laws and regulations (our political future!) can look different.

And I want to bring my food community along. To say, "Hey, if we were as savvy as big food companies, then local food could have just as big of an impact on our local laws and policies."

Small food doesn't lobby. And we have disparate fights. We're siloed. But if we pull it all together, we could really shake things up. gc

Rising from the Rubble:

By Elazar Sontag
Photography by Ana Lorenzana

Finding Community through Misfortune

"My biggest quality is that I'm really stubborn," Norma Listman says, letting out a belly laugh. But she's not joking. Norma's perseverance has propelled her through the endless challenges of opening a restaurant—many of which she couldn't have prepared for.

Norma launched Masala y Maíz in Mexico City last year, with her partner, Saqib Keval, a fellow chef and activist. It's an experimental restaurant and research kitchen where the flavors of Saqib's Indian and East African background collide with those of Norma's Mexican heritage. A deeply personal project for both Norma and Saqib, the restaurant was on track to be a huge success, receiving bundles of praise and media attention. But a massive earthquake and a corrupt government official's personal grudge stopped the restaurant from opening—twice. Now Norma is depending on the strength of her community to keep the restaurant's spirit alive.

Norma was born in Texcoco, just northeast of Mexico City, and spent seventeen years in Oakland, California, where she worked in art galleries and managed some of the city's most loved restaurants, including Camino and Bay Wolf.

Norma's interest in food started when she was a girl, spending her free time with her grandmother. "Not in a conventional way of spending hours in the kitchen with the pots and pans and my grandma," she clarifies. On the weekends, Norma, her aunt, and her grandmother would get on

153

I wanted to be here working, creating jobs, and trying to change things.

a bus or a train and visit the churches of surrounding towns. For her grandmother, these trips were a chance to feel close to God. For Norma, they were all about what happened after the praying was finished and they would head to the market. "You understand the diversity of who we are in the markets," Norma says. In Michoacán, there were *uchepos*—sweet, fluffy tamales. In Hidalgo, Norma found the best barbacoa. She fell in love not just with Mexican food, but its history, too.

Norma moved to Oakland on a whim in 1999, after falling in love with the city's art and music scene. When she wanted to start cooking professionally, she found some restaurants to train in, and began hosting her own events. Over the years, she noticed the American chefs she worked with becoming increasingly interested in Mexico's heirloom corn varieties. Norma's father works for the International Maize and Wheat Improvement Center (CIMMYT) in Texcoco, so she was aware of the country's corn varieties long before they found an audience in the States. "This is the essence of my culture," she says. "Corn is more than a crop for us. Corn dictates our cosmology."

Both Norma's American and Mexican friends voiced their concerns when she talked about going back to Mexico. There was too much corruption, they believed, to successfully run a restaurant there. The corruption, Norma knew, was real, but she also knew she couldn't have any impact when she was two thousand miles away. "I wanted to be here working, creating jobs,

and trying to change things," she says. Any challenges that might come her way, she was ready to face.

After moving to Mexico City, Norma was offered a space to open her business. The design was already gorgeous, with an equipped kitchen where she could research and develop recipes, and a living space to host chefs-in-residence. Within two weeks of her move, Norma was paying rent. Saqib joined her a few weeks later, and they were on track to open their restaurant. Masala y Maíz's menu—jumbo shrimp seasoned with a housemade masala spice blend and served with jicama and peanuts; thin, fermented-rice tortillas topped with pickled onions and a dollop of chutney—represents the hours of shared family stories and recipe testing, which Norma and Saqib go through each time their fresh produce is delivered. "It's a very intimate dialogue between Saqib's family, my family, and our family recipes," Norma says.

After four months of renovations, menu design, and anticipation, Masala y Maíz was set to open on September 25, 2017. A week before opening day, the city was hit by an earthquake that crumpled buildings like tissue paper. The opening was put on hold. "We turned the restaurant into a community kitchen," Norma says, "and cooked eight hundred hot meals every day." The restaurant acted as a soup kitchen of sorts for more than a month. What was supposed to be the restaurant's soft opening became an effort to support those in the community who were displaced, hungry, and afraid.

An investor pulled her support after the

earthquake, and Norma had to postpone plans to transform one of Masala y Maíz's rooms into a mill where she could research varieties of corn and their possible uses. But stubbornness continued to push Norma forward. Masala y Maíz had a chef-in-residence program—something Norma had always dreamed of—and people loved the food. Despite everything, this was a dream restaurant, a space where she could collaborate, express herself, and start important conversations about Mexican culture.

One brunch service, just as the restaurant was beginning to feel like a stable home, a construction crew started working on the sidewalk outside. The jackhammers blew dust through the restaurant's windows, and interested passersby barely glanced at the menu before moving on to quieter streets. Norma pleaded with the crew to work only when her restaurant was closed, but they refused. The construction continued for weeks, and she kept losing money. One morning, with her refrigerators stocked with fresh seafood and all her employees working, Norma reached a breaking point. She was going to have to close for the day before she had even made enough money to pay her servers and cooks. A conversation with the construction foreman quickly escalated. "You guys should watch out, because you will lose your jobs," he warned. "I hope all your paperwork is in order." Two days later, government officials shut down Masala y Maíz. The restaurant had been open for just five months.

"I'm not going to be defeated by a system," Norma says. "And it's not just me.

I'm not going to be defeated by a system. I have nine employees. I have to fight for them, too.

I have nine employees—there's two single mothers, two heads of families. I have to fight for them, too." Norma and Saqib agreed when they first opened Masala y Maíz that they were going to do things "the right way." That meant paying their taxes and social security for employees. It also meant not paying bribes. "If we do," Norma says, "we're part of a system that we want changed." For four weeks, the pair have waited to hear from government officials about the status of their case, but so far they haven't gotten any news. And unwilling to pay anyone off, Norma is not hopeful that the process will speed up.

"A lot of people don't think they have the option to not pay a bribe," Norma has realized. "It is so ingrained in Mexico that sometimes people think that it's the only way." But as Norma and Saqib fight against the shutdown, support has poured in so quickly, the pair can barely stay on top of it. Norma gets at least five calls a day from chefs offering restaurant space or volunteering to host fund-raisers for Masala y Maíz.

At Cicatriz, a nearby café, Norma and Saqib are selling *donas en el exilio*, homemade doughnuts, to raise money. Eduardo García, often praised as one of Mexico's top chefs, offered space at LALO!, one of his restaurants, for a Masala y Maíz pop-up. Recently, Elena Reygadas—Latin America's Best Female Chef in 2014—called Norma to ask how she could help. "On the one hand, I feel really fortunate receiving

these calls," Norma says. "I just wish it was under different circumstances. I understand that I wouldn't be receiving these calls right now if my restaurant wasn't closed, so it's a really sweet and sour dynamic."

The pop-ups and the doughnuts won't cover all the restaurant's costs while it's closed. Still, the support has been invaluable. "It's overwhelming, and it's very humbling," she says. "Look at the thread and the make of this community. I feel really lucky."

But as fortunate as she feels, Norma still worries. Last week, she thought the paperwork would be delivered so she could reopen Masala y Maíz. It never arrived. "I think we have a really good restaurant, but I want it to be better. I want it to be the best restaurant it can possibly be. When the best chefs in the continent are calling you and offering their space, and you're cooking for them, it's a game changer. It's a complete game changer."

Masala y Maíz would have been a success without the earthquake or the hurdles, and without being shut down. But when it does come back, it will do so with the combined support of an entire community—Mexico's best chefs, along with a group of already loyal customers, will be waiting for the doors to open. Thanks to her stubbornness and a commitment to doing things the right way, not the fast way, Norma has become part of the fabric that holds Mexico City together. **gc**

MASALA & MAÍZ

Anarchy as Antidote

At Commissary and Lagusta's Luscious in New Paltz, New York, a nonhierarchical business structure allows Lagusta Yearwood, Kate Larson, and Alexis Tellefsen to explore and collaborate on their own terms.

By Alicia Kennedy
Photography by Winnie Au

"I think about fear all the time," Lagusta Yearwood tells me as we sit down at the bright blue tables outside Commissary, the New Paltz, New York, café she co-owns. That someone as busy as she is—there's the café, the chocolate shop around the way called Lagusta's Luscious, the East Village sweets shop Confectionery, and a cookbook draft due soon—has time to consider fear is striking.

But she's able to do all that because she's ceded some power at the shops over the last few years, giving managers Kate Larson and Alexis Tellefsen room to grow their own skills and bring their talents into the café. All the mugs at Commissary were designed by Alexis, a ceramics artist; its zine library is stocked with Kate's collection, and she also books its shows.

These spaces they've built are also among the most inclusive in the Hudson Valley area, offering a special haven for queer folk. A chocolate Pride Bark flavored by a locally sourced rainbow—dried mint, lavender, raspberries, and more—currently on sale gives 20 percent of its proceeds to local friends' gender-affirming surgery funds. Yet Lagusta, Kate, and Alexis don't think they're doing enough.

"I don't feel like our workplace is as inclusive as it should be," says Lagusta. "New Paltz is kind of hard in that way."

"This town is not particularly diverse," adds Alexis. "But we do have a wide range of people, and we never limit what we want from someone we hire."

"I do think people are drawn to us because it's a place where they feel like they can be themselves," Lagusta allows, as Kate tells her, "Whether you know it or not, you make space for people to just be people."

And in a harsh world currently enduring a harsher-than-usual political climate, that's a radical ethos—which becomes even more welcoming when served with a sourdough bialy and cashew milk latte.

The four of us talked about the community and creativity they fearlessly cultivate in their small town, all while working tirelessly at their individual projects.

Anything I've ever done in business, I've never known the right way to do it, so I just did it. I'm glad about it, because how else would you do things?

How did you all end up in New Paltz?

Lagusta Yearwood: My partner and I both were living in Teaneck, New Jersey, and working in the city. I was doing a meal delivery service, so I could live anywhere so long as there were good farmers' markets. I just asked around the Union Square farmers' market: "What are good farming towns?" Someone at the market said New Paltz, and the mayor, who was in the Green Party, had just been in the news for marrying gay people illegally. I was in the Green Party—I still am—and the mayor's my age. We came up, looked at two houses, and bought one.

Kate Larson: I came to college here, and I was working a couple of other jobs, but I was a customer at the chocolate shop and saw they were hiring, and thought, *"Why don't I get a third job?"* And that's what I did. I'd always worked with vegans, because I'd always just had jobs with my friends, but I'd never worked in a space that was exclusively under that umbrella.

Alexis Tellefsen: I got a BFA in ceramics from SUNY New Paltz in December 2014. I was there a bit longer than I planned to be, and I went back home to Middletown, New York, for break. I needed a job and applied on a fluke. I'd never been there, but I applied, and now it's the biggest part of my life.

Lagusta's Luscious opened in 2011. What was that process like, and how did it grow into three businesses?

Lagusta Yearwood: I was doing this meal delivery service, also called Lagusta's Luscious, and then I started making chocolates on the side and selling them through PayPal. I just got really burnt out. I'd done the meal delivery service for nine years. The chocolates had gotten bigger and started taking over, so I had to pick one of the jobs, and I chose the one that didn't involve breaking down a case of onions every day. We opened the shop, and it grew—and I guess it's still growing, who knows? I should know that. I should have numbers!

In 2016, we opened up Commissary and Confectionery in one week.

Was there a lot of fear in that transition?

Lagusta Yearwood: Honestly, no. There wasn't a lot of fear. I think this is the theme of my whole life: If I'd thought about it, I would've been scared. I actually just got fear in my stomach thinking about how scary it was. We were like, "We'll just rent a place in Manhattan and open a shop." You just do one thing after another and look back and see that they were extremely terrifying.

But also, my mom had just died in December, and we started to open both places in March, so I was pretty much a zombie with no capacity for thinking or feeling. That worked in our favor.

Anything I've ever done in business, I've never known the right way to do it, so I just did it, and amazingly, that has worked out so far. I'm glad about it, because how else would you do things?

Did grief change your relationship to the world?

Lagusta Yearwood: It changes everything. I think being a caretaker for my mom for literally a year and watching her so slowly die—for the first time in my life, I didn't care about work, which has never happened to me. The only reason we were able to open Commissary and Confectionery is that I was able to take time away from the chocolate shop. Before that, I just figured I had to make all the chocolates, everything had to go through me, and when my mom got sick, I thought, *I don't care at all.* The shop learned to live without me. Now they don't need me at all. This place is like a whiny, two-year-old baby that constantly needs things. I always show up for our little 11:30 chocolate meeting and then do whatever, because they're fine, which is mostly because of Kate and Alexis. They do everything.

Now I owe it to everyone to pay it back. If shit happens in your life, let's make it work. We're all here for each other. Remember, Alexis, that summer you didn't know how to drive?

What's the point of being alive if you're not doing weird shit? My whole business philosophy is, "How weird can I make it? How far can I push it?"

Alexis Tellefsen: I failed my driver's test. I didn't take it until I was twenty-two. I just never drove. I was like, "Well, I might not have a job to come back to." It was never a question, though. I think prior to all the things that you went through, Lagusta, there's never any question of challenging anyone for their needs in this space. We let people be people, always.

Lagusta Yearwood: I think, for me, it's kind of a selfish business decision. We're in a small town and finding amazing people is really hard. If you're great, I'll do whatever for you.

Do you think you consciously cultivated the open, inclusive space at the shops?

Lagusta Yearwood: I feel so lucky now that I live in this super-insanely-comforting, soft, wonderful world. I've lived in a world of kindness my whole adult life. I feel so grateful for it, and I forget how special it is. I've worked really, really hard to build that, and I never want our shop to be a weird cult with all the same kind of people. For a while, people thought we didn't hire men, but we have men working here.

I try really hard to not care about making a profit—which is obvious, because I don't really make a profit—and I'm always trying to push my politics into things. What's the point of being alive if you're not doing weird shit? My whole business philosophy is, "How weird can I

make it? How far can I push it?" I'm also really lucky that I have Jacob, who's my co-owner at Commissary; Maresa, who co-owns Confectionery; and Kate, who basically co-owns the chocolate shop, though she won't because she wants to be able to go on tour with her band. The three of them always pull me back from the edge.

You are super open on social media, and it's not like following a business account at all. Is that a conscious choice and are you afraid that influences who comes here, in some way?

Lagusta Yearwood: I don't think it's a conscious choice, though with Confectionery I try to be more professional. I think it's the only way I can be. I could try really hard, but then I'd get bored and give it to someone else. It hasn't failed yet, so I'll keep on with it. But I would say it screws me over a lot of times. It is awkward because I'm not really a people person, but I've created this world where people know everything about me. You can't have it both ways. It's definitely not the best marketing decision, but I think that's why people follow us. They don't feel marketed to. I don't understand other businesses: This is your whole life, but you're doing it in such a boring way—what's the point?

How have you let that perspective influence your decision to let your

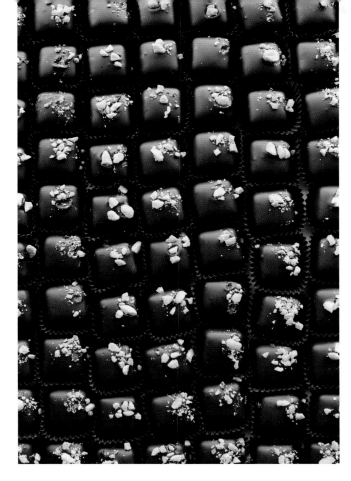

THE

mitzvah WALL

Buy anything for anyone – a small tea for your friend Maresa, a Pickle Plate for anyone who's short on cash this week, an espresso for someone wearing a New Order shirt – at the front counter. Note your mitzvah (in Yiddish, "mitzvat" means "good deed") on the paper provided, and hang it up here. If you fit the description of any of these mitzvahs, bring the paper up to the counter to claim your treat.

You want to be at a level where you're like, I'm a little scared to be where I'm at. *That's where you get your life done.*

employees bring their creative practices into their work?

Lagusta Yearwood: I'm always really ashamed that we can't pay people better and we don't have benefits, and I always think that we'll get there—though I still don't know how. The only trade-off I can offer is to make work really great. I also think that, for me, it's a good practice to get into to see other people's strengths. Because I have all these political views of anarchy and that everyone has something to contribute—all these cheesy things about seeing where people shine. I think what most jobs do is say, "Here's the job. You fit into it or you don't." What I try to do now is be like, "What's good for you? How can you best succeed in this job doing something you're good at?" It's big enough now that there's space for people to be like, "I naturally gravitate toward this."

What's it like to have a job that encourages your unrelated creativity?

Kate Larson: I guess the shop itself is a different rung of the DIY ladder in one way—people knowing they can learn from each other and have things to teach each other and you don't have to be a pro or have a book contract. My whole life, I've made zines, because it's something I knew I could do and I didn't need validation at all. I wasn't influenced by anything outside of myself, and it just made sense. Being in

the shop, we all make sense of things on our own, and it's a rare space of mostly women figuring it out as they go along, in some respects. DIY is making your own rules and trusting yourself to do it. So much of what we do at the shop is the same thing.

Alexis Tellefsen: I bought my wheel a year ago and started making ceramics out of college, and I just launched my business, Tellefsen Atelier, last year. Lagusta's been extremely supportive, and I think the community of people that I have has been extremely supportive. I wouldn't say it informs my practice as much as it does me as a human being. I feel really buoyed by my community all the time. It's also been an extremely flexible job for me. I can say, "Hey, I'm gonna take a break to go unload my kiln, half an hour away!" and everyone is very understanding. It's made me a stronger part of this community, even more so than when I was in college, so I'm getting a lot of community support and eyes on my work.

What does being fearless mean to you?

Lagusta Yearwood: Both of you are so much more fearless than I am. I can talk about ways that I think you're so fearless.

Alexis Tellefsen: I know what it's like to be fearful, to second-guess myself, to try to fit in, and I feel, for me, being fearless is just being unapologetic in who I am—to

embrace that and come into that, and recognize that with myself and my artwork, I don't have to question myself. I should embrace what I'm doing and living in any given moment, because that's who I am.

Kate Larson: I think I'm full of fear. That's what helps me live well. For me, at different times of my life, fearlessness came out of losing control—when you suddenly have the realization that things are going to happen to you that you can't do anything about, and you just have to go from there, you lose fear in your life because you're more focused on "What can I do?" You're not focused on what you should be afraid of, but instead on how you can fill in the gaps. Fearlessness is just not giving yourself the choice to feel fear.

Lagusta Yearwood: You don't want to just go through your days thinking, *I feel completely confident. I'm working at my exact level.* You want to be at a level where you're like, *I'm a little scared to be where I'm at.* That's where you get your life done. **gc**

to buy
UDON
NOODLE
spinach pesto,
spicy tofu
no gluten
SALA
SALAD
slaw
lettuce, mustard
ASK
WHAT
ALL
$12
RSVP
shiitake
cooked
optional
RICE

Sharing Space for Dream-Chasing

Coworking Spaces Offer Women and Non-Binary Creatives a Place to Be Fearless in Pursuit of Their Goals

By Kelli Hart Kehler

We are living in a time that feels both transformative and still massively archaic—the businesses and careers of women and non-binary people are multiplying and thriving, coming into the light in a brave and bold way. But the gender wage gap as of 2017 was 18.2 percent—an example that the greater part of society does not view women or non-binary people as equal to men. This construct of lopsided worthiness can leave women and non-binary people feeling less than, uncelebrated, unsupported, and even unsafe in workspaces. Recognizing this need for workplace sanctuary, a growing number of coworking spaces around the country have been specifically designed for women and non-binary creatives. In these safe, welcoming spaces, creatives can work and share with and alongside their like-minded peers, and also hunker down to work individually in a place where they feel supported, understood, and part of a community.

Here the founders from six coworking spaces specifically created for women and non-binary people share their missions behind starting these spaces, the power of community, and much more.

Why is it important to create physical spaces for women and non-binary people to work?

Ali Greenberg, The Broad (Richmond, VA): There is a rich history of women and gender minorities organizing, but so few spaces that serve them in all their needs or recognize their breadth and impact— let alone are designed with them in mind. With streets named for men, monuments of men, and institutions run by men—it is

no wonder that the shelves are too high and the offices too cold. By building our own spaces, we solve not only a representation issue, but a design one!

Bethany Iverson, The Coven (Minneapolis, MN): Most spaces we inhabit are designed for men first; they were made by men with other men in mind. Every day we watch women and non-binary folks transform after spending time in The Coven, a space designed first and foremost around their wants and needs. Being part of a space that prioritizes women and non-binary folks changes how we carry ourselves into the rest of the world—it reminds us of our power, reinforces our sense of self, and makes us feel seen and heard.

Rachel Khong, The Ruby (San Francisco, CA): I'm a writer, and writing can be isolating work. In starting The Ruby, I was interested in creating a physical space for writers, artists, and other freelancers who do solitary work; I'm all too familiar with that feeling of loneliness. I was also interested in the fact that often creativity happens when you're outside of your head, talking with other people. The internet has changed the way we work, and also the way we socialize; we're more isolated than ever, and many of us are looking for a sense of connection. I wanted to gear The Ruby specifically toward women and non-binary people because, especially in San Francisco, we aren't often the focus.

Kerra Michele Huerta, BUREAU (Washington, DC): Studies have proven time and again that women thrive professionally, emotionally, and educationally when men are removed from the equation—regardless

of the age group being studied. Don't get me wrong, I love men, but it's extremely important for women and those who identify as women to have a space they can feel "safe" in, whether that be physical safety or intellectual safety. Women are trained from a very young age that their voices aren't as loud or important as male voices, and by

Photo of The Broad by Sarah Schultz-Taylor

creating safe spaces for women, we are allowing women to develop their voices and speak louder.

Kelsey Pike, Cherry Pit Collective (Kansas City, MO): The most significant reason for creating a physical space for women to work is to bring comfort to our members. Cherry Pit Collective is a space where we feel physically safe while we work, relaxed and free to be ourselves: a sensation often challenged in male-centric workplaces. Some of the major advantages of creating a studio space for women in like fields are the sense of support from other women and the feeling of being treated fairly, things we've found to be inherent in a shared female workplace. Our original mission was to fill our studio with awesome, hardworking artists and makers. The first dozen happened to be female-identifying, which worked so well, we decided to intentionally move forward as a female collective.

Alicia Driskill, evolveHer (Chicago, IL): evolveHer is a creative workspace designed for women to connect, collaborate, and curate a life they love. evolveHer not only provides a beautiful workspace, but also offers a robust schedule of custom programming to support its community of women in all aspects of life (business development, wellness, and connections). In addition to our programming, we provide a safe space for women to talk about sensitive issues such as #MeToo and the gender gap, as well as daily challenges such as motherhood and career growth.

Can you describe some of the biggest challenges that creatives face in your city?

Ali Greenberg: Richmond is an exceptionally creative city, but that saturation means that there is an expectation of free or cheap work. Creatives here have to work hard to raise the ecosystem's valuation of their craft of service.

Liz Giel, The Coven: There are many creatives in the Twin Cities who struggle with

Photo of evolveHer by Anna Zajac

access to resources and opportunities. Education for aspiring creative minds here is a challenge, with fewer opportunities available compared to what other cities enjoy. As one example of this, Miami Ad School's Minneapolis location closed suddenly a few years ago, leaving many aspiring creatives in the lurch. In addition to this, there is a growing issue of racial disparity in our city

that creates even more significant barriers for women and non-binary creatives, who represent historically marginalized backgrounds. These individuals have a difficult time finding professional opportunities and environments where their unique experiences and talents are fully embraced. As a result, creative organizations are also suffering from a lack of diverse perspectives.

Rachel Khong: Here in San Francisco, the biggest challenge has been the rising cost of rent. It's increasingly becoming a place where creatives can't afford to live.

Kerra Michele Huerta: Washington, DC, isn't exactly known outside the District as a creative space. Those of us in the "inner circle" are very aware of the creative power this small geographical area holds, but the powers that be don't necessarily prioritize us, our needs, or art in general. It can be very difficult to get funding from investors in this area, or raise awareness for our causes, because DC is such a political town.

Alicia Driskill: Authentic connections are a huge challenge in Chicago. A lot of networking events encourage business card spamming versus truly providing an opportunity to build relationships on a deeper level. Another challenge is in the isolation aspect of being a creative. When you can surround yourself with a positive support group, you begin to gain more confidence in your work and have the opportunity to collaborate.

How does your community help creatives through some of the scariest parts of starting or running their own businesses?

Ali Greenberg: Richmond is a true community—if you have an idea, all you need to do is put it out there into the world and you will have a team behind you. Everyone is willing to help you work through the tough times, whether that be a lawyer chatting formation over a coffee or a fellow maker sharing supplier info or a friend sharing your work with a new group!

Bethany Iverson: We offer a wide array of programming and workshops to give our members access to new tools and information—right now we're focused on tackling topics like financial literacy, the new tax laws, leadership development, storytelling, and confidence. Equally important is the community we're cultivating at The Coven. Members frequently turn to other members, either in person, through our mobile app, or within our private Facebook group, with calls for help with everything from photography to copywriting to tracking down lawyers and accountants.

Rachel Khong: We're a venue for classes, events, and general fellowship. The classes, of course, can be helpful in specific, hands-on ways—we've had classes on everything from finance to makeup to wine-tasting. But one of the main resources available are the members themselves; I'm proud of the fact that The Ruby is home to an incredible pool of talented people, who are rooting for you to succeed and happy to lend their expertise.

Kerra Michele Huerta: Because BUREAU is composed almost exclusively of entrepreneurs, the women who are members are all in the exact same scary boat—and everyone is generous with life jackets! If someone voices that they're having trouble with their website, or their taxes, or their social media plan, there's always a gal ready to offer support and advice on the topic.

Kelsey Pike: Our collective is built of members with varying skill levels and backgrounds. Some of us have been running our businesses for a decade, while others are just starting out. It's our aim to learn from every member. Fresh perspectives help seasoned makers view things from a new angle, and established artists freely offer up advice to the freshmen. We encourage each other to try new things, share unique specialties with one another, and comfort each other as a resource for human connection.

Alicia Driskill: I personally sit down with each new member as part of the onboarding process to understand what they do, where their challenges are, and how we can help them get started and/or grow their business. We connect them with other members who are in similar fields and life phases. We also provide classes on a variety of creative areas such as design, copywriting, and content creation.

Photo of BUREAU by Reema Desai Boldes

What are physical aspects of your coworking community that help make people feel at home and welcome?

Ali Greenberg: The Broad was designed to feel like a living room—a comfortable and familiar place where you feel like you can put your feet up! Everything from the signage to the lighting to the bathroom

products and wallpaper were made by women in our community—members and guests can see themselves in the space!

Erinn Farrell, The Coven: We describe the layout of our space as "coffee shop–style coworking" . . . meaning, there aren't desks or offices to rent, but rather a comfy, inviting atmosphere that focuses on

community first. Our ultimate goal was to create a space that felt like a modern art museum you could put your feet up in—so we selected furniture and design elements that were bright, espoused joy, and would be comfortable for any body. In creating a space that was not only intersectional, but equitable, we spent a lot of time with community members to select art and design

How do you see your space and community growing over time to help the creatives in your area?

Ali Greenberg: The goal of The Broad is to evolve into a comprehensive headquarters for the women of Richmond and Virginia—our big vision is being ground zero for a new female-driven economy in our city and our state, so that means education, incubation, and investment!

Alex West Steinman, The Coven: Right now, our space is intentionally very artful and open with creative headspace in mind. It's a space that serves both our creative and corporate members. In addition to continuing to evolve with our community's needs in our current location, there's definitely an opportunity to expand to other locations with room for more creative studio and art rooms, individual workspaces, and more creative event spaces. We're just getting started here—the limit does not exist.

Rachel Khong: My hope is that we'll have partnerships and collaborations with other Bay Area organizations—the hope is to give back to our community and neighborhood; the hope is that The Ruby can improve not only the lives of its members, but also our city and the Bay Area as a whole. My hope is that we can be a space where books get written, and project ideas get sparked, and friendships and collaborations form. My hope is that we'll be a large enough network that the Bay Area creative community can easily find the support and help they need, in whatever form that may take.

elements that represented their heritage and larger community. We also carved out space for a Parent & Prayer room, a Self-Care room, individual phone booths, and a shower with towel service.

Kelsey Pike: Our building has several shared spaces, open to all our members, that make it feel like a cozy home. There is a kitchen and large communal eating area, a comfy lounge, and a big backyard with a fire pit. Each interior studio stall opens out to the common space, encouraging an open and kind atmosphere between studiomates. It's impossible to arrive at the studio and not see who else is working. This welcomes conversation and closeness among members.

People (and especially women and non-binary folks) crave spaces with resources to grow businesses and ideas, and opportunities to network with members. It's not enough to just have a desk—find a community.

Kerra Michele Huerta: I see BUREAU continuing to grow in membership, adding more and more ladies with different strengths and characteristics to our crew. As our membership grows, our ability to help one another grows, and our workdays and workshops are that much more productive and insightful. It takes a village, as they say, and I really believe that's true.

Kelsey Pike: We hope to grow our class offerings and to expand our reach within the Kansas City area. We want to share our members' knowledge and skills with a larger audience.

Alicia Driskill: As our community grows, our ecosystem will get even stronger. We help drive business to each other and connect women now . . . so the bigger the community, the more knowledge we can share. We have strategic partnerships in place that also provide free or discounted resources to our members.

Have you changed your space or the way you work since your opening day as a result of community feedback?

Ali Greenberg: We are constantly adapting and iterating. We run surveys every month, have completely open lines of communication with members, and are always looking at ways to improve or add to the space and our programming—including a new expansion with more flexible hours!

Erinn Farrell: Absolutely! It is our commitment to our members to gather feedback and be honest and transparent with what we are learning and how we are growing. In terms of the layout of the space, we've adjusted elements of the space to offer more standing-desk options and larger worktables to allow our members to spread out a bit more. We've also adjusted our member communications to ensure our members have plenty of heads-up on programming, and we've continually adjusted our programming to allow our members more chances to create real connections—rather than just networking.

Rachel Khong: We're brand-new and still evolving everything. There's nothing that's not still a work in progress!

Kerra Michele Huerta: Yes, definitely. What I have heard most is that people want longer opening hours, so I'm extending hours significantly from early morning to late night, and adding weekends. I hope it works out! But I honestly have no idea what I'm doing from day to day, so who knows!

Kelsey Pike: In the beginning we had trouble finding the right balance of work between our members. As the members have grown to know and trust one another and feel autonomy and agency as members of the collective, it has been increasingly easy to divide tasks based on personal interests and skills. Our members handle all aspects of managing our collective. This includes cleaning, promotional work, class programming, event coordination, and member recruitment.

What are your top three tips for people who might be scared to join a new coworking space because they don't know anyone yet? How can they connect and make genuine friends?

Ali Greenberg:
1. Remember that everyone there shares something in common! Don't think that you are the only one feeling new or out of place.

2. Just show up! Check out the programming and see what piques your interest. There is always something going!

3. Any space worth their salt will make it a priority to help you feel a part of things—don't be afraid to befriend the staff and let them know what you are looking for, whether it be the best spot to get some work done or a specific connection!

The Coven:
1. Find a community that fosters connection. Many folks need more than just a desk. People (and especially women and non-binary folks) crave spaces with resources to grow businesses and ideas, and opportunities to network with members. It's not enough to just have a desk—find a community.

Photo of The Cherry Pit Collective by Kelsey Pike

> *As our community grows, our ecosystem will get even stronger. The bigger the community, the more knowledge we can share.*

2. Go to events even if you don't have a buddy to go with! Too often we pass on attending things because we don't have a friend to go with. This is a great way to make new connections with folks interested in the same topic.

3. What makes a workspace a true community is the facilitation of connection between members. Don't be afraid to introduce yourself to the person sitting next to you! It's likely they're in an industry that's different from or complementary to yours. What a great way to learn something new, build a partnership, or create a new friend.

Rachel Khong: I've definitely been in that boat of being scared and not sure if someone wants to be friends with me. I'm very much an introvert, and I feel like it takes me a long time to get to know people. The benefit of being part of a space like this is that people are here because they're interested in knowing you and meeting new people—that's already a given. It's nice to have that as a baseline. I've been thrilled to see all the get-togethers that happen outside The Ruby, too—Ruby members making plans to get dinner, or go to a comedy show, or collaborate on a project. That makes me feel like this whole experiment is working.

Kerra Michele Huerta: I am an introvert and struggle to make new friends, so I can definitely understand being scared or nervous to start at a new space.

1. Choose a space on the smaller side. If you struggle to meet people and you join a huge coworking space, you're going to feel like a guppy in a huge aquarium. Take some time and research size and number of members before committing to a space to ensure you won't feel overwhelmed on day one.

2. Most coworking spaces offer member events so people have a chance to mix and mingle. Check out the space's online calendar or reach out to the space directly and ask if you can attend an event to see if it's a good fit for you.

3. Take the time to send a little info about yourself, what you do, and what you're into when reaching out to a space about membership. Ask them if they know of other members who have similar businesses or interests, and see if you can come in for a trial day on the same day as one or more of those people. A little extra effort on the front end can go miles in benefits in the end!

Kelsey Pike:

1. Test it out. Depending on the space, this might mean attending an event, going for a tour, or checking out open studio hours.

2. Be your authentic self from day one. If you want real connections, don't waste time with small talk. These are people you may be spending a lot of time with; give them the opportunity to really get to know you and be a support system for you as well.

3. Once you're in, really spend time there. You won't make friends if you don't show up for real face-to-face time. If applicable, try volunteering in a way that will make you a valuable member of the space.

Alicia Driskill: I hear a lot that people are scared to come to networking events by themselves, but when they do, they look down at their watch two hours later and realize how many amazing women they've met and how much fun they're having. So I would say:

1. You can't grow in your comfort zone. Get out of your own way and take the step.

2. Read the company's mission and what they stand for and see if it resonates with you. When you read our manifesto, you know exactly what we stand for.

3. Look for a space that invites you in and introduces you to others. By getting to know our members personally, we're able to connect them with others at events so they can start to develop deeper relationships. **gc**

INFORMATION

THE COVEN

MINNEAPOLIS, MN

The Coven is a collaborative community and coworking space designed with women and non-binary folks in mind.

Website: thecovenmpls.com
Instagram: @thecovenmpls

THE RUBY

SAN FRANCISCO, CA

The Ruby is an arts & letters–focused work and gathering space for creative Bay Area women of all definitions.

Website: therubysf.com
Instagram: @therubysf

BUREAU

WASHINGTON, DC

BUREAU is a boutique, members-only coworking space in the Adams Morgan neighborhood of NW Washington, DC. Designed with entrepreneurs in mind, BUREAU serves as a sanctuary for women to network, collaborate, and share ideas. This designer space is also available for private events, and hosts monthly gatherings and workshops for members and the community to come together.

Website: bureau.studio
Instagram: @bureaustudio

CHERRY PIT COLLECTIVE

KANSAS CITY, MO

Our communal art space is a 1,500-square-foot light-filled remodeled warehouse building. The original exposed-brick walls and functional support beams convey a sentiment of industrialism and craftsmanship. Today, the building houses about a dozen female makers. We emphasize collaboration and community and prioritize the voices of the marginalized.

Website: cherrypitcollective.com
Instagram: @cherry_pit_collective

THE BROAD

RICHMOND, VA

The Broad is a workspace and social club for women and gender minorities in Richmond, Virginia. The first space of its kind in the state of Virginia, The Broad's coworking facilities during the 9-to-5 allow for a productive workday, while curated events and programs in the evenings cater to the diverse interests of a growing community.

Website: wethebroad.com
Instagram: @wethebroad

EVOLVEHER

CHICAGO, IL

evolveHer is a creative workspace designed for women to connect, collaborate, and curate a life they love. evolveHer not only provides a beautiful workspace, but also offers a robust schedule of custom programming to support its community of women in all aspects of life (business development, wellness, and connections). The 5,000-square-foot River North loft was intentionally designed to inspire creativity and serves as a unique space to host off-sites, private events, and trainings.

Website: evolveher.community
Instagram: @evolveher

Additional coworking/community spaces designed for women and non-binary creatives:

Femology
Detroit, MI
femologydetroit.com

The Hivery
Mill Valley, CA
thehivery.com

Ladies Room
Chicago, IL
ladiesroomchicago.com

The Lemon Collective
Washington, DC
wearethelemoncollective.com

Let's Vibe
Chicago, IL
letsvibe.org

New Women Space
Brooklyn, NY
newwomenspace.com

Pastel Plymouth
Plymouth, MI
pastelplymouth.com

The Riveter
Seattle, WA
theriveter.co

Women's Center for Creative Work
Los Angeles, CA
womenscenterfor creativework.com

Zora's House
Columbus, OH
zorashouse.com

Library of Congress Cataloging-in-Publication Data is on file.

ISBN 978-1-57965-861-8

Design by McCalman.Co
George McCalman, Aliena Cameron

Artisan books are available at special discounts when purchased in bulk for premiums and sales promotions as well as for fund-raising or educational use. Special editions or book excerpts also can be created to specification. For details, contact the Special Sales Director at the address below, or send an e-mail to specialmarkets@workman.com.

For speaking engagements, contact speakersbureau@workman.com.

Published by Artisan
A division of Workman Publishing Co., Inc.
225 Varick Street
New York, NY 10014-4381
artisanbooks.com

Artisan is a registered trademark of Workman Publishing Co., Inc.

Published simultaneously in Canada by Thomas Allen & Son, Limited

Printed in the United States

First printing, October 2018

10 9 8 7 6 5 4 3 2 1